Staffing Tomorrow's Parishes

Experiences and Issues in Evolving Forms of Pastoral Leadership

Maurice L. Monette, Editor

Sheed & Ward

ISBN: 1-55612-366-3

Published by: Sheed & Ward
                  115 E. Armour Blvd. P.O. Box 419492
                  Kansas City, MO 64141-6492

To order, call: (800) 333-7373

Contents

Symposium Participants

Sr. Marcia Allen, CSJ	Concordia, KS
Rev. James Baker	Diocese of Dodge City, KS
Most Rev. Lawrence A. Burke, SJ	Diocese of Nassau, Bahamas
Rev. Tom Caroluzza	Diocese of Richmond, VA
Sr. Mary Donard Collins, BVM	Des Moines, IA
Rev. Owen Connolly	Archdiocese of Halifax, CANADA
Most Rev. Joseph P. Delaney	Diocese of Fort Worth, TX
Sr. Rosemary Dilli	National Pastoral Life Center
Most Rev. John F. Donoghue	Diocese of Charlotte, NC
Most Rev. John J. Fitzpatrick	Diocese of Brownsville, TX
Most Rev. George K. Fitzsimmons	Diocese of Salina, KS
Most Rev. David Foley	Diocese of Richmond, VA
Most Rev. Gerald A. Gettelfinger	Diocese of Evansville, IN
Sr. Mary Kay Hadican, CSJ	St. Louis, MO
Most Rev. William R. Houck	Diocese of Jackson, MS
Rt. Rev. James Jones, OSB, Abbot	Conception Abbey, MO
Most Rev. Raymond A. Lucker	Diocese of New Ulm, MN
Most Rev. Andrew J. McDonald	Diocese of Little Rock, AR
Rev. Steven C. Moore	Archdiocese of Anchorage, AK
Most Rev. Thomas J. Murphy	Archdiocese of Seattle, WA
Most Rev. James D. Niedergeses	Diocese of Nashville, TN
Most Rev. Anthony J. O'Connell	Diocese of Knoxville, TN
Msgr. Patrick J. O'Keefe	Diocese of San Bernardino, CA
Most Rev. Bernard F. Popp	Archdiocese of San Antonio, TX
Mr. Tony Raskob	RASKOB Foundation
Rev. Gary Reller	Natl Federation of Priests' Councils
Chaplain Robert Richter	U.S. Army, Washington, DC
Most Rev. Francis X. Rogue	Archdiocese of Military Vicariate
Rev. Frank Ruff, GHM	Superior General of Glenmary
Chaplain Donald Shea	Chief of Army Chaplains, Wash., DC
Most Rev. Michael J. Sheehan	Diocese of Lubbock, TX
Very Rev. Edward J. Slattery	Extension Society, Chicago, IL
Rev. John F. Slattery	Diocese of Colorado Springs, CO
Rev. Charles J. Strelick	Diocese of Marquette, MI
Most Rev. John J. Sullivan	Diocese of Kansas City-St. Joseph, MO
Rev. Thomas Tank	Archdiocese of Kansas City, KS
Jean Marie Hiesberger	Director, IPL
Hugh J. McCabe	Director of Development, IPL
Thomas D. Frary	Assistant Director, IPL
Joan R. DeMerchant	Associate Director, IPL
Catherine Jantsch Butel	Associate Director, IPL

Preface

Over the past several years, the Institute for Pastoral Life has responded to continuing requests to help dioceses deal with the phenomenon of parishes without a resident priest. As this phenomenon matured, a number of requests came from bishops and other principal decision-makers for a forum in which to discuss and reflect upon some of the current approaches to staffing parishes experiencing this reality. Some bishops were interested in discussing with others their own experience of alternative staffing; others wanted to learn more about what was happening in these dioceses and parishes to better prepare themselves for the not-too-distant future.

The decision was made to conduct a symposium focused in particular on the phenomenon of the Parish Life Coordinator (as persons in this pastoral role are sometimes called). For over a decade in some places, religious women and men, lay ministers and/or permanent deacons have been appointed to oversee faith communities, and the number of persons in this role has increased steadily in the past several years. The time seemed ripe to explore what has been learned from this experience and what are the key issues that have surfaced as a result of this staffing approach. The symposium, "Parish Leadership in Light of the Diminishing Number of Priests" took place in October, 1989 to explore these critical questions. This book describes and analyzes the symposium and its findings.

This symposium, however, did not occur in a vacuum. It was one of a series of responses initiated by IPL since its inception in the mid-'80s. The Institute inaugurated a summer training program in 1987 for persons appointed to or preparing for pastoring roles in parishes and missions without a resident priest. It has gathered and published guidelines, policies and job descriptions developed by numerous dioceses for alternate forms of pastoral leadership. In addition, IPL hosted two other invitational symposia: one focused on assisting priests who work with Parish Life Coordinators and the other directed toward parishes in the transition to new forms of pastoral leadership. Print and video resources were developed out of these symposia; some of them are listed in the bibliography of this book.

The symposium, "Parish Leadership in Light of the Diminishing Number of Priests," and this book have been made possible through the generous funding of the Raskob Foundation. The event was planned by the staff of the Institute for Pastoral Life and was designed and facilitated by Maureen Gallagher. Several persons from across the United States shared their pastoral experience at the symposium. They were: S. Elaine Byrne, OSU, Pastoral Associate in the Diocese of Owensboro; S. Kay Fernholz, SSND, Pastoral Administrator in the Diocese of New Ulm; Rev. William Spilly, pastor of a four-parish team from the Diocese of Rochester; Rev. Mr. Roland Benoit, Pastoral Associate, and Rev. Mr. Patrick Burke, Pastoral Administrator in the Diocese of Fort Worth; and S. Mary Jo Mutschler, SC, Director of the Greco Institute in the Diocese of Shreveport. Dr. Gary P. Burkart, Rev. Charles W. Gusmer and Rev. Berard L. Marthaler, OFMConv. presented papers that are included in this book. The Institute for Pastoral Life is grateful to all of these people and to the symposium participants for their contribution to this important project and to the future of parish ministry.

Introduction

Staffing Tomorrow's Parishes is addressed to the concerns of bishops, diocesan personnel and heads of religious congregations presently faced with major decisions about staffing parishes at a time when the number of priests in their dioceses is rapidly diminishing. Its purpose is to familiarize church ministers with the phenomenon of the parish life coordinator and to explore with them the issues involved.

What better way is there to achieve such a goal than to seek the informed opinion of bishops, diocesan officials and heads of religious congregations who have already staffed parishes with parish life coordinators? Such was the purpose of a two-day symposium held at the Institute for Pastoral Life in Kansas City, Missouri in October, 1989. Twenty-two bishops gathered and with them diocesan officials, superiors of religious congregations and experts in related fields of interest. Together they listened to parish life coordinators tell of their experience, reflected on the Tradition, explored the research of social scientists, and discussed their perceptions of the issues and strategies related to the parish life coordinator phenomenon.

The three chapters of Staffing Tomorrow's Parishes explore in detail the major findings of this conference:

- Chapter I describes the emerging role of the parish life coordinator, that is, the person (or in some cases persons) who has been chosen by an Ordinary to shepherd, in collaboration with a designated ordained pastor, a parish without a resident priest. The role is placed in the context of facts and figures related to the diminishing number of priests, the priestless Sunday phenomenon, and alternate forms of parish staffing.

• Chapter II describes the primary issues raised by the parish life coordinator phenomenon, as perceived by the participants at the October, 1989 symposium.

• Chapter III relates the symposium deliberations and the three background presentations delivered at the symposium. It offers summaries of the papers and reflections on the dialogue which ensued. These three papers, edited and expanded in response to the symposium conclusions, are included in the Appendices:

- the first reflects from the perspective of the Catholic liturgical/sacramental tradition;

- the second, from the perspective of the ecclesiological and historical tradition;

- and the third, from that of a relevant theme from the social sciences, namely "role theory."

Each of these chapters offers the reader a frame on the situation, that is, a systematic way of perceiving and analyzing the phenomenon of evolving church leadership. These papers provide a context for understanding the symposium deliberations reported in the second chapter.

The book concludes with a bibliography for those who want to deepen their understanding of the issues. Only readings most directly relevant to practice have been suggested.

Before we proceed, two items beg for clarification: the use of the term "parish life coordinator" and the tentative nature of the hypotheses in this book.

First, we clarify the term "parish life coordinator." There is actually no one way to adequately describe or name the role of the person appointed to head the parish in the absence of a resident priest. Some speak of the pastoral administrator, while others speak of the parish director, pastoral coordinator or parish life coordinator. There are other terms as well. The Institute for Pastoral Life uses the term "parish life coordinator." The term, while not perfect, does not present canonical problems.

Also variable is the name given to the priest working with the parish life coordinator: priest moderator, sacramental minister, and canonical pastor. The person in this role may or may not be the regular sacramental minister who presides at the sacraments reserved by law to the role of priest. He may be a diocesan vicar appointed as pastor to all or several of the diocesan parishes without resident priests. He may even in some cases be the bishop who has reserved for himself the role of pastor to these parishes.

This book will, for the sake of consistency, use the term "parish life coordinator" in reference to the new ministry role and "priest" in reference to the canonically appointed pastor. Would that we could find better terms! But, we are dealing with a situation in flux and we live in "in-between" times.

That brings us to the second remark. Just as there is no one way to name the roles, there is no one way to view the phenomenon of the parish life coordinator. This book is not a definitive word. It is only one attempt to name and address the issues surfacing for bishops, diocesan officials and heads of religious congregations. The data is scant. Hard research is non-existent. But church officials are faced with a diminishing number of priests and are asking non-ordained women and men and permanent deacons to assume pastoral roles in collaboration with priest-pastors.

This book is a response to church officials and others who are eager to know how those who have experience with parish life coordinators perceive the issues. It is the beginning of a dialogue that will hopefully yield suggestions on how to proactively meet this parish staffing challenge.

Chapter I

Parish Life Coordinators: Facts and Figures

The parish life coordinator phenomenon is perhaps best understood within the context of . . .

(1) the diminishing number of priests,

(2) the growing phenomenon of "priestless Sundays" and

(3) the rise of alternative forms of staffing parishes.

The present chapter explores this context and the facts and figures related to it.

The Diminishing Number of Priests

The most comprehensive study of the declining number of priests in the U.S. is that by Dean Hoge of Catholic University, *The Future of Catholic Leadership: Responses to the Priest Shortage.*[1] The following data is excerpted from that study:

- Since 1920, the number of priests increased with the steadily increasing Catholic population, that is, until 1965 when the decline began.

- The number of Catholics per priest increased from 1920 through 1985. For instance, in 1957 the ratio was 664 to 1; in 1977, 846 to 1; in 1985, 912 to 1. In 1990, the ratio stands at about 1000 to 1. The difference widens when using nationwide poll estimates rather than the above *Catholic Directory* figures.

1

• The number of seminarians grew about as rapidly as the number of Catholics until 1965. Then there occured a dramatic decline which continues till our own time.

• The drop in the number of active diocesan priests by the end of the century is predicted to continue. If 35 to 40 thousand were available in 1970, predictions are that between 15 and 20 thousand will be in the year 2000. The drop in the number of priests is even more significant if religious order priests are included, because the decline in their number is even more extreme.[2]

• The decline in the number of priests is not evenly distributed in geographical terms. It is worst in the Southwest and has not yet hit some cities in the East.

• Fr. Robert Sherry of the NCCB proposed the priest-to-laity ratio of 1975 as a minimum standard of priests needed for today: 1 to 791. By this standard, the shortage of priests in 1990 is about 13,000.

• International statistics reveal that the decline in the number of priests is also being experienced elsewhere and particularly in the industrialized nations. In France, for instance, over 22,000 parishes were without priests in 1982. In Austria, the number of parishes without resident priests tripled between 1950 and 1976. There is, however, an increase in vocations in the Third World countries of Africa, South America, the Philippines and also Poland.

Priestless Sundays

A survey released to the members of the National Conference of Catholic Bishops in 1988 by Bishop Joseph Delaney, Chairman of the Bishops' Committee on the Liturgy and a participant in the October 1989 symposium, reveals that . . .

• 51 of the 174 U.S. dioceses already face the problem of priestless Sundays "either weekly or occasionally" and 91 more "foresee such a need in 5 to 10 years."

• 70 dioceses presently have parishes/missions which are under the administration of a deacon, a lay person or a religious sister or brother.

• The number of such parishes is 193 and a total of 201 persons are involved. (The number of these parishes/missions does not add up to 193 since some persons administer more than one parish or mission, and some parishes/missions or groupings of them are administered by a team.) These persons include: 40 deacons, 125 women religious, 8 men religious (brothers), 14 laywomen and 14 laymen.

• 137 dioceses reported weekday celebrations of Holy Communion outside Mass in the absence of a priest within the past year.[3]

Models of Alternate Staffing

The 1986-87 research of the National Pastoral Life Center indicates that there are several models of alternative staffing for parishes without resident priests:

A. *Multiparish Pastors.* Assigning one priest to be the pastor of more than one small to moderate sized parish, each parish possibly having its own full-time staff.

B. *Multiparish Teams.* Assigning pastoral responsibility of two or more parishes to a team, each parish maintaining its own identity and structures, but fostering interparish programming.

C. *Parish Clusters.* Organizing groups of parishes that suffer from inadequate funds or insufficient numbers to support a good program so that their various ministries are joint efforts, e.g. joint religious education, joint councils, and cluster schools. Each parish may retain its own priest or main pastoral minister.

D. *Parish Directors.* Assigning a person who is not a priest to assume responsibility for all of parish life with the exception of those sacramental celebrations that are provided by the non-resident pastor who maintains oversight responsibility.

E. *Parishioners as Pastoral Leaders.* Assigning not an outsider but a member of the parish to assume pastoring responsibilities under the supervision of a non-resident pastor as described in Model D.[4]

Parish Life Coordinators

The appointment of a parish life coordinator or "parish director" is, according to this typology, one alternative (Model D) to using a full-time resident priest-pastor. But parish life coordinators are actually serving as alternative leaders (1) for single parishes as in Model E, as well as D, and (2) for several parishes as in Models B and C.

Sociologist Dr. Gary Burkart has identified three empirical models involving parish life coordinators:

(1) one PLC and one parish,
(2) a team and several parishes,
(3) a team and a cluster of parishes.

This classification makes more explicit the ways in which parish life coordinators function. These three models are further explored by Dr. Burkart's article in Appendix C of this book.

In conclusion, it should be apparent that there is no one model for the role of parish life coordinator. The role is exercised in many ways depending on local needs. The symposium participants heard from priests, deacons and parish life coordinators involved in five different parish situations around the country. But interestingly the participants did not dwell on the strengths and weaknesses of each type of situation, nor did they search for an ideal type to be prescribed for their dioceses. They recognized that the role of parish life coordinator is still developing and that effective prescriptive models have not yet emerged. So, the symposium participants devoted the bulk of the discussion to the deeper issues, which we explore in Chapter III of this book.

Notes

1. Sheed and Ward, 1987.

2. Studies of Richard Schoenherr, sociologist at the University of Wisconsin, quoted by Hoge, *op. cit*, pp. 7-8.

3. Source: *Newsletter* of the Bishops' Committee on the Liturgy, July/August 1988, Volume XXIV.

4. "Alternative Staffing of Parishes," in *Center Papers,* a publication of the National Pastoral Life Center (299 Elizabeth St., New York, N.Y. 10012), Number 3, Spring 1987.

Chapter II
Parish Leadership in Light of the Diminishing Number of Priests: A Symposium Report

A Scenario

Many bishops in the U.S. share the problems of this bishop: he is charged with a geographically expansive diocese with a growing but widely scattered Catholic population. The number of diocesan and religious priests available for parish assignment is rapidly diminishing and the ratio of priests to parishes is at an all time low of one priest to every two parishes. He is fortunate to have a small Catholic college in the diocese. It provides training for volunteer pastoral ministers like catechists, liturgy planners and parish council members. But the diocese has few other resources and is considered a "home mission" diocese.

This bishop sees no reason to close parishes because of the lack of priests. The parishes are actually growing and the faithful are less likely to travel very long distances to attend Mass. In fact, people have become very attached to their home parishes and have continuously expressed the preference to keep their parishes open even without a resident priest. Many more people are assuming responsibility for the ministerial functions of the parishes. Many are taking advantage of the extension courses offered by the lay ministry institute sponsored by the college.

The bishop has already appointed parish life coordinators to five of the parishes. People have grown accustomed to women and married persons in positions of authority and have commented positively on the new dimensions which these persons have brought to the liturgy and to ministy in general. Some people, however, are still asking the bishop to send them a priest.

Some of the priests are resisting the new role of non-resident pastor but many of them are now more willing to accept it—even though the role remains ambiguous in relation to that of the parish life coordinator. Some priests complain that they cannot keep pace with the amount of travel that the provision of sacramental ministry demands of them.

The bishop has met with the diocesan pastoral council and with the clergy council to discuss the staffing of parishes. He engages the councils in an exploration of staffing problems, the issues involved and the available strategies. They try to find solutions within the church's present policies which exclude the ordination of married priests, the ordination of women priests or deacons, or the appointment of persons who are not priests to preside at Eucharist.

Introduction

The symposium began with an exploration of several such scenarios described by a panel of parish life coordinators, deacons and priests. Their experiences became the starting point for reflection on the following topics:

• the positive outcomes of the diminishing number of priests and the rise of parish life coordinators,

• the key issues involved, and

• possible responses by key decision-makers.

This report summarizes the discussions on each of these topics.

Positive Outcomes

The symposium participants surfaced what, in their views, have been the positive outcomes of the phenomenon of the diminishing number of priests and the rise of parish life coordinators. These are listed below in priority order. The numbers at the end of each statement indicate the weighted score.

1. The emergence of new ministries which is permitting women and married people to add to or enhance the ministry of male celibates. (83)

2. The recognition of the need for pastoral planning. (77)

3. The recognition of the need to clarify the roles of the ordained priest and the parish life coordinator and the meaning of the "priesthood of the faithful." (60)

4. The revitalization of congregations and the activation of local leadership which has allowed small parishes to stay open. (25)

5. The manner in which parish life coordinators have created an atmosphere in which people can respond in ever-broadening ways to the baptismal call to service. (8)

6. The readiness exhibited by communities to be served by parish life coordinators (7); and, the opportunity for all to live the Paschal Mystery by dying and rising in this time of change. (7)

7. The teachable moment that is occuring for the church. (3)

Issues

The symposium participants surfaced five major issues related to the problem of staffing parishes. These are listed in priority order, the numbers at the end of each issue indicating the weighted score:

1. The relationship of sacramental care to pastoral care. (58)

2. The future of Eucharist as central to Catholic life. (52)

3. The need for clarification, communication, and collaboration at all levels. (33)

4. The investment of human and financial resources needed to move the church in the direction of training parish life coordinators. (30)

5. The clarification of the role of priest. (27)

We first examine each of the major issues, as surfaced at the symposium. Then we will list the other issues mentioned.

(1) Sacramental Ministry and Pastoral Ministry

When a parish's sacramental ministry is served by a non-resident priest and when much of the parish's pastoral ministry is served by a parish life coordinator, the parish faces both threat and opportunity concerning the unity of its ministry.

The threat arises from the virtual separation of two ministries which have traditionally been joined in the person of the priest. Questions arise, including the following: Is the fruitfulness of the Eucharist threatened when the presider is not a local resident intimately involved in the lives of the faithful and the events of the locality? How can the non-resident priest really celebrate the community life of the parish when so much of his energy is invested elsewhere? How can the priest presider not feel like a stranger when the parish life coordinator has been the one to prepare the couple for marriage, counsel the faithful coming to confession and comfort the dying now seeking the Sacrament of the Sick? If liturgy is to mirror the life of the parish and if the role of the parish life coordinator is to be reflected in liturgy as are other pastoral roles, how is the pastoral ministry of the parish life coordinator to find expression in the liturgy, especially the Eucharist? Is it desirable for parishioners and for the continuity of ministry that pastoral and sacramental care come from two perhaps disparate sources? Some would say that the separation of pastoral and sacramental leadership could serve to weaken the sacramental nature of the church and the experience of Eucharist as the source and summit of Catholic Christian life.

On the other hand, new opportunities have arisen in the sacramental/pastoral life of parishes. The parish life coordinator and the parishioners are in many places assuming their baptismal responsibility to care for each other in ever-expanding ways through pastoral ministries. Because of such emerging leadership, parishes that were threatened with closure are remaining viable. New gifts in addition to those of priests are being offered to pastoral ministry, such as the gifts of married persons and of women. Some say that a key dimension of pastoral ministry is being re-activated through the parish life coordinator, namely the ministry of building community. Furthermore, many parishioners seem to be accepting the ministry of persons other than priests. Some are even asking why parish life coordinators cannot witness their weddings, hear their confessions, anoint their sick and, in the absence of sufficient priests, preside at Eucharist.

(2) Eucharist

The second issue, the future of the Eucharist, flows from the first. Eucharist was professed by the symposium participants and by others as central to Catholic parish life.[1] The diminishing number of priests is perceived as a threat to that centrality, especially as some bishops are having more and more difficulty providing a priest for Eucharist every Sunday in every parish. Now that Eucharist has increasingly been accepted by the faithful as "the source and summit" of Christian life, the lack of priests compromises its availability. Also, the circuit riding of the non-resident priest risks the impression that Eucharist and the other sacraments are somehow magic. The preeminent position of the Eucharist as the Sunday service in Catholic parishes may be threatened by the increasing use of the Communion Service. The service is sometimes refered to by parishioners as "Sister's Mass" or the "Deacon's Mass," indicating the possibility that the distinction between Eucharist and the Communion Service may become blurred. There is also a danger that the parish life coordinators may become discouraged in trying to engage the services of a priest to minister to the community on a regular basis. If Eucharist is central to Catholic identity then it would appear that the Communion Service is not an adequate substitute for the eucharistic liturgy.

Desirable as weekly Eucharist may be for a eucharist-centered parish, some opportunities are emerging from the lack of priest presiders. For one, Communion Services and other forms of worship like Morning Prayer and The Liturgy of the Word are providing the parish with new presiders, including the laypersons, sisters and deacons delegated for that role by the bishops. As women and married persons, they bring new and different gifts to the celebrations. Their presiding affords them the opportunity to link the liturgical ministry with their pastoral ministry. There is also evidence that parishioners are accepting these new presiders. Some symposium participants expressed the desire that the Communion Service be offered in anticipation of the day when the full Eucharist with priest will be celebrated in the parish. Others suggested that the Communion Service not be used as a matter of course. Some expressed the hope that, if the Eucharist is really so central, other qualified persons will be officially commissioned to preside. Others suggested that the building of a community that is eucharistic is a strategically prior concern to the provision of a presider for Eucharist. How normatively desirable, they ask, is a parish that has multiple Eucharists each Sunday yet demonstrates little eucharistic community life as evidenced in the quality of pastoral care and mission to the world?

So, questions remain in the minds of symposium participants, including the following: If Eucharist is central to parish life, how can it be provided every week as is the custom? Should Eucharist be provided every week? Should the official church allow bishops to delegate persons other than priests as eucharistic presiders? What are the long-term advantages and disadvantages of the Communion Service?

(3) Communication, Collaboration and Clarification

The third issue that the symposium participants identified arises from the ambiguity and confusion engendered by (1) the diminishing number of priests; (2) the Vatican II teachings regarding the participation of all baptized in the priesthood of the faithful; and (3) the many kinds of alternative staffing arrangements that have recently emerged.

The participants were concerned, in the first instance, that priests and parish life coordinators communicate and collaborate effectively as they struggle to identify their emerging roles.[2] They also expressed concern about emerging models for alternative staffing, including those that involve parish life coordinators. They are aware that these models are still in early stages of development.[3] But the discussion did not dwell on these two concerns. Instead, it focused on more foundational concerns like . . .

• The function and role of priesthood. What is the proper role of the priest today? Which functions belong exclusively to the priestly role and which does the priest share with other ministers and parishioners?

• Catholic identity and the overall mission of the church: What specifically is the mission of the church in U.S. society? What is central to Catholic identity within this mission? What are the objectives of that mission today and what functions are needed for the achievement of those objectives? What roles are needed to carry out those functions?

• The proper function and role of the parish and other Christian communities within that mission: Is the parish the appropriate structure for achieving the mission of the church in today's society? Might the parish be more effective when it functions as a gathering of smaller Christian communities? What roles are appropriate in such a setting?

Some participants said that they would be grateful for an influx of priests which would obviate the question of alternative staffing and the re-examination of these foundational issues. In that spirit, a few publicly advocated daily prayer for priestly vocations. But, for the most part the assembled participants did not forsee an immediate end to the staffing crisis and so expressed intense concern about the foundational issues described above.

In that light, many participants advocated strategic planning processes at all levels of the church:

- "strategic" in the sense that the processes facilitate a reexamination of the foundational issues and a projection of plans that can be successfully implemented in the forseeable future; and

- "at all church levels" because the facing of issues and the projection of plans on each of the levels effects those on every other level, be it parish, diocesan, national or universal.

Participants recognized that the problem being faced in the home mission dioceses is yet to be felt in the more priest-filled areas like the Northeast. But they stressed the urgency of their situation in priest-poor dioceses and they recognized their dependence on the National Conference of Catholic Bishops for policy formulation in certain critical areas. Among these areas of needed policy mentioned are . . .

- the role of the priest,

- the ministerial roles open to women,

- the proper role of the deacon,

- the nature of the parish in function of the mission of the church,

- the appointment of persons other than priests and deacons for the administering of sacraments,

- the compensation of pastoral ministers,

- the allocation of national and regional resources for the nurture and training of newly developed ministries, and

- the development of pastoral plans to meet the needs of new immigrant groups like those from the Orient and Latin America.

One group at the symposium suggested that home mission bishops bring issues such as these before the NCCB and propose the appointment of advisory groups for such purposes as the development of education and formation centers and the formulation of policies for living wages, personnel selection, retention and termination.

(4) Human and Financial Resources

How willing is the church to do the work described in issue #3 and to invest the human and financial resources needed to move the church in the direction of trained parish life coordinators?

The symposium participants felt that such commitment is necessary if the needs of priest-poor dioceses are to be effectively met by qualified parish life coordinators. They perceived the issue as a national issue requiring action on the part of the National Conference of Catholic Bishops. Such action would include naming and claiming the need for alternative forms of parish leadership, establishing the need as a priority, allocating educational resources, and establishing just wage policies.

(5) The Clarification of the Role of Priest

Priestly role clarification surfaced in the formulation of several of the key issues, but it also emerged as a key issue in itself. Vatican II documents addressed the role of bishops and the role of the faithful, both in terms of ministry within the Church and mission to society. But the documents did little to clarify the role of the priest. This situation has engendered a role confusion about priesthood not unlike that about the parish life coordinator role. There is no universal clarity about the structurally given demands associated with the position. The way priests conceive of their role varies widely, as does their performance. The new role of parish life coordinator further complicates the matter. Who is the priest in relation to the parish life coordinator? Who is he in relation to the parish in which he is non-resident pastor? In this role, how should he relate to the bishop? What is the role of the priest in relation to pastoral and sacramental ministry?

Other Issues

Several other issues surfaced during the symposium:

• the preservation of authenticity of faith and doctrine, especially the Eucharist; (9)

• the absence of minority groups in this symposium; (9)

• the need to define the mission of the parish; (8)

• the relationship of the parish life coordinator to the priest; (6)

• the need to decide if parish life coordinators are "bishop extenders" or "priest extenders"; (3)[4]

• the need for parish life coordinators to encourage priestly vocations; (3)

• the need to study and resolve power issues; (2)

• the need to address the morale of priests and their sense of fragmentation. (2)

Responses to the Positive Outcomes and to the Issues

At the end of the symposium, with little time remaining, small groups of participants surfaced strategies to enhance the positive outcomes and constructively face the critical issues surrounding the phenomenon of changing parish structures and authority positions. The strategies which surfaced were not prioritized, nor were all the participants of the symposium involved in ratifying each idea. The summary which follows represents the work of six small groups of participants who spent forty-five minutes generating ideas for possible action based on the top priorities under "positive outcomes" and under "critical issues."

Positive Outcome: The emergence of new ministries which is permitting women and married people to add to or enhance the ministry of male celibates.

Three major sorts of strategies emerged from the groups considering how to enhance this positive outcome:

The first was the issuing of a pastoral letter by the NCCB. This letter would present a vision of ministry and describe the possibilities and opportunities for new forms of ministry. Local bishops could then issue their own diocesan statements which would identify concrete situations in which laity and religious could utilize their gifts and training in full and part-time ministries.

A second suggestion was that the Institute for Pastoral Life develop a paper based on this symposium which would focus on the roles of ordained priests, parish life coordinators and "the priesthood of the faithful." This document could be used as a working paper until the NCCB might produce a pastoral on ministry. Participating dioceses could use the document to facilitate role clarification.

A final set of strategies was educational in nature. It was suggested that dioceses develop ministry training programs, catechetical materials, and study days on the theme of ministry.

Positive Outcome: The recognition of the need for pastoral planning.

Both groups working on this question suggested that dioceses develop pastoral plans based on mission statements clarifying the role of the diocese in relation to parishes, the mission of parishes, and the centrality of Eucharist. Such planning would be broad-based, involving input from parishes and research from other dioceses. Planning was also suggested for the national and provincial or regional levels.

Positive Outcome: The recognition of the need to clarify the roles of the ordained priest and the parish life coordinator and the meaning of the "priesthood of the faithful."

Suggestions focused primarily on the clarification of "role demands," that is the structurally given demands associated with a given social position. Accordingly, dioceses (and the Vatican and the NCCB) would clarify "job descriptions" or responsibilities and develop appropriate training programs.

Issue: The relationship of sacramental care to pastoral care.

The one group that responded to this issue wrestled with the distinction between pastoral ministry and sacramental ministry and surfaced definitions of their own. In the end, they suggested that the NCCB, local bishops and diocesan and parish councils wrestle further with the question. No concrete suggestions emerged regarding how this should take place.

Issue: The future of Eucharist as central to catholic life.

Each of the two groups that discussed this issue surfaced similar suggestions. To quote:

> "Bishops must dare to address the question of who presides at the community's Eucharist."

> "Somehow the opportunity to discuss the implications of changing the marital and gender requirements for candidates for ordained priesthood should be opened up by the bishops."

Other strategies included . . .

> • Bishops encouraging the Bishop's Committee on the Liturgy to produce a document on the importance of eucharistic unity in light of the declining numbers of ordained ministers.

• Parish ministers and parishioners dividing large parishes into small faith-sharing communities (if true community is to be the appropriate setting for eucharistic celebration).

• Parish life coordinators using their strategic position to build small communities by calling forth local leadership, involving more and more people in parish life and preparing them for eucharistic celebration.

• The Institute for Pastoral Life sponsoring a seminar and commissioning papers to address critical issues like the future of Eucharist.

Issue: The investment of human and financial resources needed to move the church in the direction of training parish life coordinators

This issue was addressed in relation to the role of the NCCB and the role of the dioceses and parishes.

Firstly, it was suggested that home mission bishops move the cause before the NCCB, so that the NCCB . . .

• name and claim the issue of parish life coordinators;

• accept the need for alternative forms of worship and identify the models which can be supported;

• agree to support alternative forms of leadership on par with candidates to the priesthood;

• assign responsibility to an advisory group to develop education and formation centers and recommend policy for family living wages, personnel selection, retention and termination;

• recommend moving away from stand-alone seminaries and encourage the formation of the ordained in the mainstream of American life or at least with all others with whom they will work in ministry.

Secondly, it was suggested that the local diocese name the pastoral needs and gifts of the diocese, discern models for effective pastoral care, and finance parish life coordinators.

The suggestions offered above were not sufficiently elaborated at the symposium because of time constraints. They are included here simply to stimulate the reader's own reflections on needed strategies.

Tensions

Participants in the symposium on the parish staffing crisis were not in full agreement about either their perception of the problem or their response. Several tensions surfaced; among them, the following:

• While some recognized the eagerness of laity to engage in the new ministries, others were more skeptical about actual lay initiative to participate.

• While some prefered that ministers be chosen on the basis of functional competence (how well they do the work), others emphasized organizational status (the fact that they belong to an officially recognized group of ministers).

• While some prefered immediate decisions that would give closure to role ambiguity, others perceived that the church (and society itself) is living in an age when roles will continue to shift as will the needs that call them forth.

• While some of those calling for control on the part of the NCCB were seeking to encourage emerging ministries, others were calling for control so as to refreeze the former organizational role and status of the clergy.

Conclusion

What might all of these deliberations mean for practice? Responses vary widely.

In order to deal with the issues around the staffing crisis, a few of the participants have already initiated diocesan strategic planning processes. With the help of diocesan staff and parish personnel, they have identified the diocesan mission, specified objectives and delineated the functions and roles needed to actualize the mission. Yet more of the participants have developed guidelines, policies and procedures appropriate to the role of parish life coordinator as it has emerged in their respective dioceses.[5]

But other participants in the symposium have been more hesitant about such elaborate planning processes. Recognizing the evolving character of ministry in today's church, they have prefered not to impose structures that would short circuit development. As one person put it, "Let it be slush!"—that is, allow the new ministries to develop organically, without the interference of blueprints from above.

Notes

1.   "Recent Roman documents testify to the centrality of the Eucharist in parish life, just short of articulating a right of the people to Sunday Mass." —Fr. Gusmer backs up his statement by quoting the canons on Eucharist beginning with canon 897. Fr. Marthaler states from an ecclesiological point of view that "the church must be seen as the primordial sacrament of the Risen Christ, a visible reality that witnesses to the working of the Spirit in the world" and that "it is first and foremost in the Eucharist that the Christian community discovers itself to be the sacrament of Christ's presence in the world." See their papers in the appendix.

2.   To assist the bishops in this task, the Institute for Pastoral Life has held a symposium and produced a video and a book entitled *Partners in Ministry: Priests in Collaboration with Pastoral Life Coor-*

dinators (Sheed and Ward, 1988). These resources report on the findings of a symposium discussion with five successful teams of bishop, priest and pastoral life coordinator. They deal with four sets of issues and strategies: leadership, identity, collaboration and structures.

3. See Chapter I of this volume for further data.

4. The "extender" metaphor was introduced to the symposium by Dr. Gary Burkhart. The parish life coordinator phenomenon, he said, bears a striking resemblance to the phenomenon of physician extender in the health care field. Physician extenders came about basically to supplement the role of medical doctor in two critically short areas of delivery, namely the inner city and rural areas. The issue raised by the participants is whether the parish life coordinator is to be conceived as a priest extender or bishop extender. The choice determines the immediate source of authority and the nature and function of the role. Is the parish life coordinator primarily responsible to the bishop or to the priest? Is the parish life coordinator supplementing the role of the bishop or that of the priest?

5. IPL has collected the work done by these dioceses across the country. The book includes examples of placement policies, training programs, job descriptions, hiring procedures, installation ceremonies and accountability procedures.

Chapter III
The Symposium Presentations

The symposium agenda included three presentations which contextualized and elaborated the dialogue among the participants. These presentations, edited and expanded in response to the symposium conclusions, are included in the appendix of this book. The present chapter reflects on the linkage between the symposium deliberations and the three papers.

Reflections from Ecclesiology and Church History

"Are there any precedents for parish life coordinators?" "What can be learned from these past experiences?" These are the questions addressed in the paper by Fr. Berard Marthaler, historian and professor of Religion and Religious Education at The Catholic University of America.

Yes, says Fr. Marthaler, there are precedents to parish life coordinators. One of these occured in Hungary during the 16th and 17th centuries. In this little known chapter of church history, during a period when church harassment by the Turks resulted in a critical shortage of priests, bishops licensed school-masters and others to undertake the entire supervision of the parish and to cooperate with religious and priests from neighboring parishes who presided at Mass and administered other sacraments. These *licentiati*, as they were called, were vital to the institutional church for over 150 years. Eventually the *licentiati* were replaced by priests, principally because they were not adequately prepared for the tasks assigned to them and also because many ordinaries regarded them as a provisional solution to a temporary shortage of priests.

This historical precedent is a backdrop for a paper which provides a theological and historical perspective from which to view the ministry of the parish life coordinator. Fr. Marthaler offers a series of principles based on theology and church history and some broad generalizations regarding the local church. He concludes with a presentation of issues raised by the parish life coordinator model and a few cautions regarding the effectiveness and survival of the model.

What follows is a summary of Fr. Marthaler's reflections in relation to the dialogue which ensued with the symposium participants:

A fruitful reflection on the *licentiati* and on the parish life coordinator or any ministerial role, says Fr. Marthaler, can take place only in the broad context of the church's mission. The nature of the church, in his view, is to be the sacramental body of Christ, a witness to the Kingdom of God and the working of the Spirit in the world. Its mission, consequently, is to proclaim the gospel message and to provide a place where the liberating and healing presence of Christ can be experienced. In the Eucharist, the church discovers its identity, preeminently so at the traditional celebration of Sunday. The Eucharist is the responsibility of the "holy priesthood" (1Pet 2:5), that is, of all those baptized in Jesus Christ and who share in his ministry and mission.

The symposium reflection on the role of the parish life coordinator proceded within the context of the church's mission as advocated by Fr. Marthaler. In fact, as previously mentioned, the participants' overriding concerns were not about models for alternative staffing and similar practical issues, but about Catholic identity, the overall mission of the church, the roles of the various ministers and the proper role and function of the parish.

Fr. Marthaler's paper also traces the major historical developments of the church's organizational structures and ministerial roles, among them: the variety in the early church, the emergence in the second century of the pattern of bishop/priest/and deacon that we know today, the increasing role of third century presbyters as presiders and pastors of local church communities, and the rise of deacons and deaconesses (more prominent in the Eastern churches). The forms and functions of these offices in the local church evolved only gradually into the seven institutionalized ministries (the major and minor orders) which were officially recognized from the 12th century until Pope Paul 1V's refinement in *Ministeria Quaedam*. This need-based understanding of the development of ministerial roles (form following function) undergirded the concerns of some of the symposium participants. They suggested that the church define the new roles of the parish life coordinator, the priest and all parish ministers in terms of the functions required to meet the needs of the priest-poor dioceses.

Fr. Marthaler speaks of the local church or the parish in the words of *Christifideles Laici*, 26, as "a community" and not principally as a structure, territory or building. While circumstances and physiognomy of parishes differ greatly, their one common denominator consists in being a community properly suited for celebrating the Eucharist. Their governance has evolved over the centuries and their ministry has taken on new forms and structures. Thus it is conceivable, in Fr. Marthaler's view, that the office of parish life coordinator as established by canon 517 could be institutionalized. In the context of the principles elaborated thus far, Fr. Marthaler raises several issues about the parish life coordinator model. He believes that the most fundamental issue is the call for a better understanding of ministry in general and Holy Orders in particular.

Who is the *de facto* leader of the local community? Is the parish life coordinator model a stop-gap measure until there are enough priests to staff present parishes and establish new ones? Is the model good in itself? Is the office of parish life coordinator a harbinger of future change? These concerns were also raised by the symposium participants when they identified as key the need to define the relation of sacramental care to pastoral care (Issue 1), the need for clarification, communication and collaboration at all levels (Issue 3); and the need to clarify the role of priest (Issue 5).

Fr. Marthaler sees much that is positive about the parish life coordinator model, including the shouldering of greater responsibility by members of the local church for the spiritual and temporal well-being of the community, the new forms of collaboration among parishes, the more direct bonds that are being forged with the bishop in the absence of a resident priest, and the emerging role of women in parish leadership. This listing was expanded by the symposium reflection and resulted in the "positive outcomes" presented in Chapter II.

Fr. Marthaler's main reservation regarding the parish life coordinator model is in relation to the provision of the Eucharist. *Ad hoc* arrangements for Sunday Eucharist and other sacraments are unsatisfactory since in his view the sacraments are essential to Catholic spirituality, and Catholic identity centers on the Eucharist. This same reservation was echoed by the symposium participants. They agreed on the centrality of Eucharist and identified the future of Eucharist as a key issue (Issue #2).

Although Fr. Marthaler's overall reaction to the parish life coordinator model is generally positive, he cautions against abuses: the absentee pastor and the raising of false expectations about the parish life coordinator role when not understood in collaboration with other ministerial roles. The success or failure of the model, he says, depends on its acceptance by both the local community and by the church at large.

Reflections from Sacramental Theology

The second presenter at the symposium was Fr. Charles Gusmer, Professor of Sacramental Theology and Liturgy at Immaculate Conception Seminary at Seton Hall. Fr. Gusmer's paper presents the view that the pastoral questions which arise from the lack of ordained priests are largely questions of identity. The paper focuses specifically on the sacramental/liturgical identities of the priest and the parish life coordinator. In Fr. Gusmer's words,

Although many administrative and financial chores which formerly accrued to the priest were never intrinsic to the ordained priesthood, there still needs to be a proper integration of the sacramental/liturgical ministry into the rest of their presbyteral ministry of serving spiritual leadership. At the same time, the ministry of the parish life coordinator needs to be properly recognized and its role within the Body of Christ properly defined. And an even more critical issue is what will happen to the Sunday eucharistic assembly when "priestless parishes" become "priestless Sundays."

In response to the leadership crisis of today's church, Fr. Gusmer, agreeing with Fr. Marthaler and the symposium participants, reaffirms the centrality of the Eucharist in parish life (Issue #2). He too is concerned that the acute shortage of priests is not going to make the Sunday eucharistic assembly a possibility for many Catholic Christians here or abroad, as is happening in countries like Zaire and Chile.

Citing a survey that indicates widespread dissatisfaction with the "half a Mass" that is the communion service, Fr. Gusmer addresses four key issues and suggests that the church take them seriously:

1. The difference between the Mass and the Sunday communion service. Echoing the words of the *Directory for Sunday Celebrations in the Absence of a Priest*, Fr. Gusmer suggests that the faithful be taught the substitutional character of these celebrations. He also suggests that priests discontinue the practice of distributing communion from the tabernacle instead of from the elements consecrated at the altar. He echoes the perspective of others that to avoid confusion a far better solution would be to keep the Sunday assembly with the Liturgy of the Hours and the Lectionary readings, but to omit communion.

2. Erosion of the ministerial priesthood. He cautions against coping with the shortage of priests by the creation of new ministries with the resulting role confusion of both. This was a complicated question for the symposium. In the end participants called for a

clarification of the role of the priest and of the parish life coordinator. Dr. Burkart addresses this issue from a sociological perspective in his paper.

3. The value of the word of God. Fr. Gusmer expresses concern that the exclusive use of the communion service may imply that the presence of the Lord in the Word has to be complemented by the sacrament in order to be sufficient. The Sunday communion service, in his perspective, is unfortunately neither a celebration of the Word nor a eucharistic celebration. Furthermore, it has little basis in tradition, having only first appeared in post-war East Germany.

4. The integral understanding of the Eucharist. The Eucharist is more than Holy Communion. The sacramental forms of the Lord's body and blood received at Holy Communion need to be seen as the fruit of the whole eucharistic action of memorial sacrifice. The communion service, in Fr. Gusmer's view, fails to convey this more theologically sound perspective.

The symposium participants echoed Fr, Gusmer's concerns especially while formulating the key issues. The separation of sacramental care from pastoral care was perceived as a threat to the unity of ministry (Issue #1). But participants also perceived in the present confusion the challenge to extend the exercise of both pastoral and sacramental ministries to all the baptized and particularly to women. In the end, questions remained as to how the Eucharist can be provided every week as is the custom, whether the Eucharist should be provided every week, and whether the official church should allow bishops to delegate non-priests as eucharistic presiders.

Reflections from a Sociological Perspective

For Dr. Gary Burkart, the church today is a "beautiful example of a social structure in evolution." Professor of Sociology at Benedictine College in Atchison, KS, Dr. Burkart offers the tools and concepts of his discipline, especially role theory, to make sense of and guide this process. "Role" typically has three meanings in social science: structurally-given demands associated with a given social position (like that of priest or parish life coordinator); a person's conception of the part he or she enacts in a group; and the actions of individual members as they participate in structured group life. Dr. Burkart contends that, with the emerging shortage of ordained pastors, these three elements of a role may be highly incongruent. Organizational demands may not mesh well with the individual's conception of the new role of priest or parish life coordinator and the individual's role actions are not likely to be consistent with both the person's role conception and the bureaucratic role demands. The resulting ambiguity for both the corporate church and individual members may lead to unsatisfying personal relations, poor group performance, job dissatisfaction, burnout and membership termination, low organizational efficiency and effectiveness, and group conflict.

Dr. Burkart echoes the concerns of the symposium participants when he calls for a greater congruence between the three elements of a role outlined above. This means that the church needs to clarify its stance on PLC's and define demands it wishes to place on the role. The process may necessitate the clarification of other roles such as bishop, priest, pastor, ordination, and parish. Dioceses may also need to develop diocesan plans to meet pastoral needs and clear policies on hiring, screening, salary, benefits and the like. Dr. Burkart's paper also offers a model for effective parish transition from priest to parish life coordinator. Four steps are suggested: diagnosing the problem, assessing the parish for change, implementing the change process, and institutionalizing the change. His paper elaborates these in detail.

As is evident in Chapter II of this book, the symposium participants made frequent use of Dr. Burkart's language and insights. They highlighted as positive outcomes of the parish life coordinator phenomenon the recognition of the need for pastoral planning and the recognition of the need for role clarification. They further agreed with him that among the major issues involved are clarification, communication and collaboration at all levels of the church; the clarification of the role of priest; and the allocation of human and financial resources needed to move the church in the direction of trained parish life coordinators. If the participants' response to his presentation is any indication, Dr. Burkart's paper will be a very helpful resource for churches attempting to respond to these issues on a practical level.

Conclusion

This chapter attempted to capture some of the connections between the symposium deliberations and the presentations of the three specialists. For a richer appreciation of the dialogue, the reader is invited to savor the text of the papers reproduced in the Appendices of this book.

Conclusion

The work at the symposium described in this book was by no means routine. Participants faced challenges uncharted by policy makers and theoreticians. Indeed, they deliberated about outcomes, issues and strategies responding to a new situation never before encountered by the church in quite the same way. But the church has been around for a long time, and now is not the first time that it has had to deal with an adaptive, that is, nonroutine problem. In fact, the very ministerial structure of the church has often been in flux, as ' some believe it is today. In the earliest centuries of the church, for instance, we have little evidence that presbyters normally presided at Eucharist. We know that, during the time of Ignatius of Antioch, bishops were often selected from among the deacons who, in fact, were the most active group of functionaries in the church. But we are not sure exactly who presided at Eucharist. Was there a split at that time between pastoral ministry and sacramental ministry? Did a broad spectrum of the faithful share in the ministerial responsibility of the church? Ignatius's conception of the local church was built on his vision of the community gathered around the eucharistic table (a concept like the one many of the symposium participants articulated). But, only later did that community have a clearly defined role of eucharistic presidency.

After the Peace of Constantine, in small Greek and Roman cities, the number of Christians was multiplying rapidly and new churches were being founded to accommodate them. Their sheer numbers precluded their gathering on Sunday around the single altar of the bishop. So, bishops began to delegate presbyters, who until now had functioned mainly as a support group and advisory council to the bishop, to preside at eucharistic celebrations in the suburban areas. Their services, however, were not always as highly esteemed by the people as those of the bishop (like today's services by parish life coordinators). So began the practice of commingling. A piece of consecrated bread from the bishop's altar was commingled with the wine on the altar of the presbyter.

This gesture was instituted in part to demonstrate the connection between the presbyter's Mass and that of the bishop. The fourth century indeed became "the century of the presbyter, the century when the presbyter's quasi-episcopal role, as delegated head of the neighborhood community or parish, became established".[1] The new role for the presbyter found an ally in one no less famous than Jerome. After correctly pointing out that the New Testament uses "presbyter" and *episkopos* interchangeably, he asks, "What can a bishop do that a presbyter cannot except ordination?"[2] Apparently, the need for role clarification we experience today is not new to our church.

The ministerial structure of the church had shifted before Constantine and has shifted since. Like the time of Constantine, ours is a time of crisis and re-evaluation.

This book has stated the issues related to this crisis as perceived by one group of bishops and other church administrators who minister in priest-poor dioceses where some parishes are staffed by parish life coordinators. The first chapter presented the facts and figures. The second chapter explored the views of three scholars on the ecclesiological, sacramental/liturgical and sociological dimensions of these issues. The final chapter reported the key responses of the participants to these issues.

If the symposium participants did not leave with definite action responses to the issues, at least they left with clearer questions.

This book will have served its purpose if the reader has also emerged with more lucid questions about the church's staffing crisis and the new role of parish life coordinator. The Institute for Pastoral Life welcomes your reactions.

Notes

1. Bryan E. Daley, S.J., "The Ministry of the Disciples: Historical Reflections on the Role of Religious Priests," *Theological Studies* 48 (1987), p. 612. This article offers a succinct summary of the historical development of diocesan and religious priesthood. See also the historical and ecclesiological perspective on ministry offered by Berard Marthaler, OFM Conv., in Chapter II of this book.

2. See Daley, *op cit*, p. 612, footnote 25.

Appendix A

Parish Life Coordinators: Reflections from Ecclesiology and Church History

Berard L. Marthaler

My assignment is to reflect on the ministry of Parish Life Coordinators (a.k.a. Pastoral Administrators). My reflections are grounded not so much on theory (what might or should be), but on practice—what in fact is. Even before we had a title for them, men and women who had assumed roles of pastoral leadership in local churches had begun to provide job descriptions based on their experiences. Everyone recognizes that the Church in the U.S. (not to mention other countries) faces a critical shortage of ordained ministers. There is no point in belaboring the fact or groping for causes to explain the decline in the number of priests, but it is important that we analyze the situation and weigh alternative forms of pastoral ministry and service. Words written by Pope Paul VI regarding social conditions seem to apply here:

> It is up to Christian communities to analyze with objectivity the situation that is proper to their own country, to shed on it the light of the gospel's unalterable words, to draw principles of reflection, norms of judgment and directives of action from the social teaching of the Church.[1]

Parish Life Coordinators are found coast to coast, from the Northeast to the Southwest, in ever increasing numbers. They staff relatively small parishes and frequently find themselves isolated by distance and misunderstandings regarding their work. Published reports and individual interviews indicate that there are occupational hazards, challenges and frustrations that seem to go with the position.[2] Since Parish Life Coordinatorss (PLCs) are pioneering new approaches and travelling uncharted paths, they are in search of acceptance, guidance, and support from other ministers in the church.

Are there any precedents for Parish Life Coordinators? What can be learned from them? It is with an eye to answering these questions, that I have been asked to situate the form and function of their ministry in the broad context of ecclesiology and to assess them in the light of historical precedents and current needs in the Church.

I begin by recounting a little known chapter in Church history that seems relevant to the discussion. Then, to provide a perspective from which to view the ministry of the Parish Life Coordinator, I outline a series of principles based on theology and Church history, and offer some broad generalizations regarding the local church. Finally I highlight issues raised by the PLC model and offer a number of cautions if the model is to be effective and survive.

The Licentiati in Hungary: A Little Known Chapter in Church History

For a period of 150 years (1528-1683), large parts of Hungary were under the domination of the Ottoman Turks. Turkish policy towards the Church alternated between harassment and persecution, restricted the movement of bishops and priests, and as a result created a critical shortage of priests. The response of the bishops was to enlist laymen to provide pastoral care.[3]

At first, the bishops commissioned schoolmasters to read the Sunday gospels and explain them by reciting sermons from approved books. In time bishops began to "license" the schoolmasters and others to baptize, witness marriages, bless the bride, catechize children and adults, preside at prayer services, lead the rosary, organize processions, and conduct funerals (with sermon). In short, they were asked to undertake the entire pastoral supervision of the parish, including the correction of public sinners and exhortations to receive the sacraments at Easter time. It fell to priests from neighboring parishes and religious to say Mass and administer other sacraments.

These pastoral administrators were licensed (*licentiati*) for a designated period, usually one or two years at a time. Thus the documents commonly refer to them as "licentiati," "fratres licentiati," "plebani licentiati" or "parochi licentiati." (The Turks called them "half-priests"!) Willibald Grasso, a Benedictine abbot of the time, composed a set of instructions for the licentiati, describing the exercise of their office and their style of life. Since the licentiati "are in a certain sense pastors," so the abbot begins his instructions, they must set a good example, avoiding drunkenness, cursing, quarrelsomeness, enmities and contentions. Every licentiatus should choose a neighboring priest as a confessor and have recourse to him for advice and counsel in the care of souls. To have his license renewed, the licentiatus had, at Easter time, to submit to an examination regarding his knowledge of doctrine and was required to show that he confessed and received the Eucharist regularly. It was customary in some places to install the licentiati in a solemn manner, but the provisional character of their commission was also impressed on them. Their official dress was a black cassock and a surplice.

The licentiati received the income and stole fees connected with their duties, but they were generally assigned to small parishes with meager resources. Their status differed slightly from place to place. In some dioceses they took part in local synods. In Transylvania they had the *privilegium immunitatis* granted to the Catholic clergy (that is, they were immune from the jurisdiction of civil courts), and those who were no longer able to perform their duties because of illness or age enjoyed this privilege, as did their widows, for life.

"The fact that the institution remained unchanged for over a century and a half," writes Eggemann, "shows its vitality."[4] But why didn't it endure?

First, it should be noted that after the shortage of priests was alleviated some parishes retained the licentiati because they could (or would) not pay the higher salary necessary to attract an ordained pastor. In one place, it is reported, the people refused a priests because they did not want to support a pastor *and* a schoolmaster.

Second, the bishops were not of one mind about the licentiati. Ordinaries regarded them as a provisional solution to a temporary problem. Many employed licentiati because they had to. Even Cardinal Pazmany, better disposed toward them than most, complained to the Papal Nuncio at Vienna, "The dismissal of the licentiates would give free hand to the Calvinistic preachers . . . The installation of licentiates, however, entails great dangers, and so I must choose the lesser of two evils." The fear in abandoning the field to Reform preachers was a major factor in appointing licentiati, but the bishops intended to dismiss them as soon as there was no longer a dearth of priests.

Third, the principal reason that the licentiati did not survive was that they were not adequately prepared for the tasks assigned to them. Some were able men, praised for their learning and dedication, but many were quarrelsome, unstable and ignorant of doctrine as well as Church discipline. Some, "for an appropriate fee," were said to witness marriages with little concern whether the parties were free to marry. Competent laymen did not find the penurious conditions of rural ministry any more attractive than priests. The bishops might have been able, had they wished, to institutionalize the licentiati by taking steps to see that they were properly trained and received adequate compensation. They preferred, however, to focus their efforts on attracting and training priests. Ultimately, their success spelled the demise of the licentiati.

The Church and Eucharist

A fruitful reflection on the position of the licentiatus, the role of the Parish Life Coordinators—or any form of ministry for that matter—can take place only in the broad context of the Church's mission. The underlying issue is not structures and organization, but the very nature of Church. The New Testament and Catholic tradition use a variety of images and metaphors to describe the Church because it is a mystery that cannot be circumscribed by definitions or captured by theological explanations. Of late it is customary to speak of models of Church, but whether one uses metaphors or models, the Church must be seen as the primordial sacrament of the Risen Christ, a visible reality that witnesses to the working of the Spirit in the world.

The Christian community, as the sacramental body of Christ, is called to be a sign of the kingdom of God in and for the world. Its mission is to proclaim the gospel message and to provide a place where the liberating and healing presence of Christ can be experienced. As such, the Church exists, not for itself, but to serve and to be the *communio sanctorum*—the place where people, called to be holy, share holy things.

The Church is visible in the Christian community. As a community of believers, made one with Christ through baptism, the Church is not a refuge from a sinful world. Rather, it is an assembly of worshipping, serving people who, while sinners, witness to the mercy of God in Christ Jesus. Through the power of the Spirit, they are called to mediate the saving ministry of Jesus to all peoples, who share a common Father and Savior. It is the Church's task to enlighten the minds of people, to enkindle love in their hearts, to heal division, and to mediate justice and mercy.

It is first and foremost in the Eucharist that the Christian community discovers itself to be the sacrament of Christ's presence in the world. It is in the eucharistic celebration that all the ministries of the Church intersect. The Eucharist incorporates ministry of the word that calls people to repentance, proclaims the kingdom to be at hand, and echoes the message of the prophets to do justice and bring peace. The Eucharist celebrates the Passover and recalls Jesus' own passage from death to life. The Eucharist is always a communal event wherein believers witness to their shared faith and commitment to the person and mission of Jesus.

The identity of the Christian community and the Eucharist are closely linked to the celebration of Sunday, which already in the New Testament is referred to as the "Lord's Day" (Rv 1:10; Acts 20:7-12). When the first Christians gathered on Sunday they set themselves apart from others: Sunday was not a day of rest in the Greek or Roman calendar, nor was it the same as the Jewish Sabbath. St. Ignatius of Antioch pointed out, "Christians no longer observe the Sabbath Day, but live according to the Lord's Day, on which our life was restored through Jesus Christ and his death." By common consensus (*sensus fidelium*), the faithful have always held the Lord's Day in such high regard that Christians have gone to extraordinary lengths to observe it as a holy day, even in the face of persecution and in the midst of cultures alien or hostile to the Catholic faith. Vatican II stated,

> On this day Christ's faithful must gather so that by hearing the word of God and taking part in the Eucharist, they may call to mind the passion, resurrection and glorification of the Lord Jesus and may thank God, who "has begotten them again unto a living hope through the resurrection of Jesus Christ from the dead" (1 Pt 2:3). [SC, 106]

Pope Paul VI stated that the ideal Sunday observance must always include "the celebration of the sacrifice of the Mass, the only true actualization of the Lord's paschal mystery."

The notion of Church, the celebration of the Eucharist and the experience of the presence of the Risen Lord are so intertwined in the New Testament accounts that it is impossible to discern which came first. Church, Eucharist and faith in the Resurrection are experiences shared in and by the community of believers. Thus when we speak of the Church's mission and ministry in the world, we are speaking of the responsibility of the whole Church and not simply of one or another group of individuals within it. Prior to any distinction of roles or offices in the Church, Christians stand in solidarity as "'a chosen race, a royal priesthood, a holy nation, a people [God] claims for his own to proclaim the glorious works' of the One who called you from darkness into his marvelous light" (1 Pet 2:9).

When the New Testament speaks of priesthood, it refers first to the fullness of the one priesthood of Christ. From this derives the priesthood that belongs to all who have been baptized in Christ Jesus. "You too are living stones, built as an edifice of spirit, into a holy priesthood, offering spiritual sacrifices acceptable to God through Jesus Christ" (1 Pet 2:5). Therefore, when we speak of the ministry and mission of the Church, we speak of the priestly tasks that are entrusted to the whole community of the baptized.

Nonetheless, there of necessity must be some distribution of labor. Despite Paul's personal desire to be "all things to all men" (1 Cor 9:22), he acknowledged that individuals have different gifts and are called to different ministries. "There are different works but the same God who accomplishes all of them in everyone. To each person the manifestation of the Spirit is given for the common good" (1 Cor 12:6-7). In his early epistles, he lists a variety of ministries and works without, however, describing how they are structured and organized. In the pastoral epistles that bear his name—1 and 2 Timothy and Titus—Paul mentions bishops, presbyters, deacons and deaconesses; he describes their personal qualifications in some detail, but is rather general about the tasks they perform.

Evolution of Ministry and Ministries

The New Testament uses a bewildering list of terms to describe ministries, a fact that indicates they were somewhat in flux for several decades.[5] The organizational structures of the local churches varied from place to place, but early in the second century the uniform pattern that we know today began to emerge. Presiding over the Christian community in each city was a leader who came to be known as the bishop or supervisor (Greek = *episkopos*). In great metropolitan centers like Rome and Alexandria, the bishop exercised his office in collaboration with a board of presbyters or elders. He presided over the liturgy—baptism, Eucharist—sanctioned marriages, and had the responsibility of seeing to it that the faithful were properly catechized. It should be emphasized that the bishops, because they exercised the leadership ministry in the community, had the responsibility for safeguarding the integrity of the Word and presiding over the celebration of the Eucharist, and not visa versa. By the beginning of the third century the episcopal office provided pastoral leadership and was the focal point of the local church.

In the course of time the number and size of the churches increased, and the responsibilities of the individual presbyters increased. The growth of the Christian community in large cities necessitated the establishment of satellite churches under the care of presbyters or, as they came to be called, priests.[6] When the great persecutions, especially in the third century, targeted bishops and forced them into hiding, priests assumed new responsibilities. In addition to preparing catechumens for baptism, instructing the faithful and reconciling penitents, presbyters began to preside at eucharistic celebrations, whereas previously their role was limited to concelebrating with the bishop. The presbyter became the *de facto* pastor of a local community. The role of the presbyter-pastor, therefore, seems to have developed differently from that of the episkopos-pastor. The latter, as noted above, presided over the baptismal and eucharistic liturgies because he was the leader; the presbyter seems to have become recognized as the leader of the community because he presided over the liturgies.

Similarly the role of deacons gradually emerged to something like that we know today. From the beginning deacons had a prominent part in the temporal administration of the churches. As assistants to the bishops, it fell to them to watch over external discipline and manage the temporal affairs of the Church, especially seeing that the poor were cared for. In the baptismal liturgy they accompanied the catechumens into the font, and at the Eucharist they read the Scriptures. Even in large churches, Rome included, it was customary to limit the number of deacons to seven, doubtless in imitation of the seven appointed to care for Greek-speaking members of the Jerusalem Church (Acts 6:1-6).

Frequent mention is made of deaconesses in the early literature, but they seem to have enjoyed more prominence in the churches of the East than in the West. The deaconesses instructed women catechumens and assisted at their baptism. They kept order in the women's section of the liturgical assembly and were present when bishops, priests, or deacons had reason to interview women. In some communities deaconesses are known to have read the Scriptures in liturgical celebrations and to have administered the Eucharist to women.[7]

The point is, the form and function of offices in the local church evolved only gradually. Jesus founded the Church, but he did not leave a blueprint as to how it was to be structured and governed. Over time, particular needs and circumstances caused some ministries to be institutionalized in new offices and under new titles. One of the earliest ministries to be given formal recognition was that of lector, an office that has endured over the centuries. The division of labor, moreover, differed from place to place and according to need. The Eastern Church recognized the ministry of the singer (*psaltes*) as did the Church in Gaul (psalmist). In the course of time, offices have been abolished and institutionalized ministries reorganized. So, for example, the office of *fossor* (literally, "grave digger"), once charged with burial of the dead, no longer exists. By the twelfth century most Latin theologians and canonists recognized seven institutionalized ministries that were divided into "major Orders" (priest, deacon, subdeacon) and "minor Orders" (acolyte, exorcist, lector, porter). This taxonomy stood until Pope Paul VI promulgated the motu prorio, *Ministeria quaedam*, abolishing the office of the subdeacon and redefining Orders and ministry.

The Local Church

The presbyteral *tituli* marked the beginning of parish churches in the third century. Even when these particular churches gained autonomy, however, they were always seen in relation to the Church universal. Diocesan and parochial churches are not simply fragments of the universal Church, nor is the universal Church a mere network of local churches. Each local church has its own integrity and manifests itself as a eucharistic community. On the model of the universal Church, every eucharistic community, if it is authentically Church, is distinguished by unity, holiness, catholicity and apostolic witness.

No sound ecclesiology can be constructed without giving serious attention to the nature, function and structure of the local church. In the wake of the 1987 Synod of Bishops, Pope John Paul II wrote,

> It is necessary that in the light of the faith all rediscover the true meaning of the parish, that is, the place where the very "mystery" of the Church is present and at work, even if at times it is lacking persons and means, even if at other times it might be scattered over vast territories or almost not to be found in crowded and chaotic modern sections of cities. The parish is not principally a structure, a territory or a building, but rather "the family of God, a fellowship afire with a unifying spirit," a "familial and welcoming home," the "community of the faithful." Plainly and simply, the parish is founded on a theological reality, because it is a eucharistic community. This means that the parish is a community properly suited for celebrating the Eucharist, the living source for its upbuilding and the sacramental bond of its being in full communion with the whole Church. Such suitableness is rooted in the fact that the parish is a community of faith and an organic community, that is, constituted by the ordained ministers and other Christians, in which the pastor—who represents the bishop—is the hierarchical bond with the entire particular church (*Christifideles Laici*, 26).

Pope John Paul, who has visited countless churches throughout the world, recognizes that the circumstances and physiognomy of parishes differ greatly. No two are exactly the same. Their one common denominator consists in being "a community properly suited for celebrating the Eucharist."

In light of history, it is evident that the governance of local churches has evolved over the centuries, and ministry has taken on new forms and structures. The Revised Code of Canon Law (1983) makes allowance for further evolution:

> If because of a shortage of priests, the diocesan bishop has judged that a deacon or some other person who is not a priest, or a community of persons, should be entrusted with a share in the exercise of the pastoral care of a parish, he is to appoint some priest, who, with the power and faculties of a parish priest, will direct the pastoral care (c. 517).

Thus it is conceivable that the office of Parish Life Coordinator could be institutionalized. Change seems to be more the norm that the exception. As it is, PLCs find themselves expected to offer services on an *ad hoc* basic that in times past have been the responsibility of deacons, priests and even bishops. Some PLCs began as catechists, some as administrators of the temporal good of the parish, some as members of a team, only to find in time they have become full time pastors. They do sacramental preparation for marriage and baptism, they conduct wake services and funerals, they visit the sick and counsel troubled consciences. They serve regularly as lectors, eucharistic ministers, and leaders in prayer services. They coordinate the ministries of other members and groups in the parish community. Though not ordained (deacons, excepted), they are expected to contract the services of a priest for the sacrament of Penance, Anointing of the Sick, Sunday liturgy and at other times when the occasion calls for it. In short, they have been given the responsibility of overseeing the local church as it seeks to grow as a community of shared faith.

Issues

The fundamental issue raised by the PLC model of the parish calls for a better understanding of ministry in general and Holy Orders in particular. In the ancient Church and for many centuries, the one who presided over the community—the bishop as an individual or in collaboration with the presbyterate—presided over the Eucharist. Although the essential link between the functions of the episcopate and presbyterate was lost sight of in the Middle Ages, only ordained ministers—priests—presided over the eucharistic assembly. In the PLC model, who is the *de facto* leader in the local community: the president of the parish council? the Parish Life Coordinator? In any case, it is not the priest who comes in only for Sunday Mass and on other occasions when an ordained celebrant is called for.

As a practical issue, one must ask whether the PLC model of parish ministry is a stop-gap measure until there are enough priests to staff present parishes and establish new ones; whether it has a particular function in small parishes and is good in itself; or whether the office of PLC is a harbinger of further change. In the latter case, the PLC model might well represent a transitional stage on our way to new parish organization and structures.

In calling for parish renewal, Pope John Paul instructed "local ecclesastical authorities" to foster "adaptation of parish structures according to the full flexibility granted by canon law, especially in promoting participation by the lay faithful in pastoral responsibilities" (*ibid*). The attractive feature of the PLC model is that it has begun to exploit this flexibility: the members of the local church are shouldering greater responsibility for the spiritual and temporal well-being of the community; new forms of collaboration are being developed among parishes; and more direct bonds are being forged with the bishop in the absence of a resident priest.

The PLC model in its present stage of development seems to be etching out, on a day to day basis, a leadership role for women. The acceptance of women as pastors in fact if not in name will in time be an important consideration in the on-going discussion over ordination. Another question, however, that is too little discussed, asks, "do ordained priests have a *collegial* responsibility for the sacramental ministry?" If, as I believe, we do, the old concept of the presbyterate, acting in consort with the bishop, needs to be renewed.

It is in relationship to the Sunday Eucharist that my principal reservation regarding the PLC model surfaces.[8] Something more than *ad hoc* arrangements for Sunday liturgy and other sacraments seems necessary if the parish is to be truly a eucharistic community. It seems to me there is danger that the Parish Life Coordinator (or whoever it is that has the responsibility) could become discouraged in trying to engage the services of an ordained priest to minister to the community on a regular basis. The sacraments are essential to Catholic spirituality, and Catholic identity centers on the Eucharist. "No Christian community is ever built up unless it has its roots and center in the eucharistic liturgy" (*Pres. Ord.*, 6). The guidelines for the Sunday assembly in the absence of a priest make it clear that prayer and reflection centered on the lectionary, even in conjunction with a Communion service, is not an adequate substitute for the eucharistic liturgy.[9]

Cautions

My overall reaction to the PLC model is generally positive because I think it offers much promise, especially in rural communities. There are, however, in addition to the Hungarian *licentiati*, two other precedents that provide cautions against possible abuses. The first is the example of the absentee pastor in the late middle ages. It was not uncommon for priests never to visit the communities they were assigned to serve as pastors. Some pastors (usually well connected in the patronage system) were even allowed to hold the office in more than one parish, without taking up residence in any of them. They neglected their pastoral charge of preaching and instructing in the faith, while delegating the sacramental ministry to poorly qualified "Mass priests" who had little or no commitment to the local community. Absenteeism was one of the grievances that fed into the Protestant reform movement. If the Parish Life Coordinator allows him or herself to be regarded as a surrogate, a stand-in for "the real" pastor who resides in a neighboring community or the chancery office, we shall have a modern version of absenteeism that is little better than the form abrogated by the Council of Trent.

The other precedent is the sacristan in a movie of the 1950s, "God Has Need of Men," or as it was known in a later release, "The Isle of Sinners."[10] An island off the coast of Brittany, placed under interdict for some reason or other by the bishop, lost its pastor. The people began to look to the sacristan to minister to their spiritual needs. He found himself imitating the priest, doing the things that he had seen the pastor do. He started modestly enough, taking care of the church property, visiting the sick; then he gave benediction with the Blessed Sacrament, and finally in a climatic scene, rather reluctantly absolved a frightened penitent who had confessed her infidelity to him. I offer the example of the sacristan to caution PLCs against simply imitating the model of the priest-pastor that can only foster false expectations on the part of the community. The Parish Life Coordinator must rather rethink his or her role and refine the new model in collaboration with the ministry of others in the community.

Ultimately the success or failure of the model depends on its acceptance not simply by the local community but by the Church at large. The bishop, in collaboration with the various councils and presbyterate of the diocese, must show support for Parish Life Coordinators: first, by arranging some kind of formal installation to give official recognition to the PLC; second, by publishing directives and guidelines that explain how the PLC fits into diocesan structures; and third, by recognizing the professional status of the PLC with regard to compensation, living situation and working conditions. The diocesan guidelines should give positive and realistic direction in spelling out what is expected of the PLCs, and outline some general principles of pastoral theology that will be of practical help in their ministry.

Finally, and above all, the people need to be made aware that circumstances are forcing the Church to develop new organization and forms of ministry. Most people are well-intentioned and can be expected to respond in a reasonable manner when they understand the seriousness of a situation. Like it or not, they recognize that change is all about: the school systems are constantly being reorganized; the delivery of medical services is in a constant state of flux; blue-chip corporations are being bought and sold and new styles of management introduced; government deregulation of the telephone company and airlines have made themselves felt at every level. Because the Church is *incarnate*, which is to say historically conditioned, it is not immune from what is happening about it. One of the strengths of the Catholic Church is its adaptability. Guided by the Spirit, it has been able to respond to changing conditions by modifying its own structures and methods. The Church now, as in the past, is exploring new means and models of ministry while keeping its eyes firmly fixed on its divinely given mission to witness to the kingdom in the world.

Notes

1. *Octogesima Adveniens,* a. 4.

2. See *National Catholic Reporter,* August 29, 1986. Peter Gilmour, *The Emerging Pastor: Non-ordained Catholic Pastors.* Kansas City, MO: Sheed and Ward, 1986. "Priestless Parishes in Western Europe," *Pro Mundi Vita: Dossiers* (June, 1979).

3. See H.J. Eggemann, "Lay Apostolate in Hungary under Turkish Sovereignty," *Social Justice Review* 40 (Jan., 1948): 299-303; (Feb., 1948): 337-340. Eggemann summarizes the research of Coloman Juhasz as reported in *Theologie und Glaube* 27:3 (1935): 322-36.

4. Eggemann, p. 338.

5. For an overview of the evolution of ministries, see Kenan Osborne, *Priesthood. A History of the Ordained Ministry in the Roman Catholic Church.* New York/Mahwah: Paulist Press, 1989.

6. The English word "priest" complicates the discussion because it translates both *presbyteros* ("elder") and *sacerdos,* the Old Testament name for the Jewish priest. The early church used *sacerdos* allegorically and, at first, only for the bishop. See E. Schillebeeckx, *Ministry,* pp. 48-50. Osborne notes that the concept of "elder" is deeply rooted in Jewish tradition, pp. 46-47.

7. See H. Frohnhofen, "Women Deacons in the Early Church," *Theology Digest* 34:2 (Summer, 1987): 149-53.

8. Much has been written on this topic. For a good discussion of the issues and an up-to-date bibliography see William Marrevee, "Priestless Masses'—At What Cost?" in *Église et Théologie* 19 (1988): 207-222.

9. *Origins,* Oct. 20, 1988; 18-34.

10. *Dieu a besoin des hommes.* Transcontinental Films, 1950. Based on a novel by Henri Queffelec.

Appendix B
The Parish Life Coordinator: Reflections from Sacramental Theology

Rev. Charles W. Gusmer, S.T.D.

Various local churches are responding to an acute pastoral need. The scarcity of ordained priests resulting in the phenomenon of "priestless parishes" has led to the development of the ministry of the parish life coordinator (PLC). Rather than closing parishes, many local churches are courageously endeavoring to preserve the traditional faith communities for as long as possible.

Theology reflects on our lived experience from a faith vision rooted in scripture and the tradition of the Church. Often a pastoral need can be an impetus to further theological reflection. In this instance we see the Holy Spirit at work calling forth leaders of local communities with the creation of a new ministry to meet a vital need. At the same time the local faith communities are challenged to a greater sense of participation and ownership in making this necessary adjustment.

But this situation raises serious problems, which have already been noted by Dean Hoge.[1]

1. Specific Issues

These issues include the divorce of liturgical leadership from enabling leadership, the identity of the PLC, and the identity of the Sunday supply priest.

a. Separation of liturgical leadership from enabling leadership

There is a separation between the pastoral leadership exercised by the PLC and the eucharistic leadership entrusted to the priest who is often available only for Sunday Mass and the other sacramental celebrations entrusted to presbyters. The use of terms such as "sacramental minister" or "celebrant" to describe the priest seems to belie this separation. In the long run all this could serve to weaken the sacramental nature of the Church when the Sunday eucharistic assembly is presided over by a presbyter without any ongoing relationship to the community. Will the Eucharist still be seen and experienced as the source and summit of Catholic Christian life?

b. Lay ministers feel hindered in their ministry by Church law and tradition

It is true canon 517/#2 of the new Code makes provisions for the PLC. But what is envisioned as an extraordinary provision is becoming more and more an ordinary reality in the life of many dioceses. One senses the justifiable uneasiness and dissatisfaction of PLCs who resent the restrictions placed on their sacramental ministry or who find themselves as pastors of a community in everything but name. Happily, they can draw support and encouragement from the diocesan church which endorses their new ministry.

c. Experience of priests cast into a "circuit riding" role, extrinsic to the ongoing life of the parish

This development could lead to a dislocation of the role of the presbyter traditionally entrusted with the ministry of word, sacrament, and pastoral leadership. The priestly ministry could be reduced to a disproportionate or exclusive sacramental ministry with no time left for the ministry of the word or shepherding. A more proper starting point for articulating a theology of the ministerial priesthood would be to see an enabling, facilitating, empowering pastoral leadership in *persona Christi* which builds up the body of Christ in its locality by word and sacrament, especially through the Eucharist, the sacrament of the unity of the Church.

To summarize, the root problem is the lack of ordained priests and the resulting pastoral questions which are largely issues of identity: the identity of the ordained priest and the identity of the PLC. Although many administrative and financial chores which formerly accrued to the priest were never intrinsic to the ordained priesthood, there still needs to be a proper integration of the sacramental/liturgical ministry into the rest of their presbyteral ministry of serving spiritual leadership. At the same time, the ministry of PLC needs to be properly recognized and its role within the Body of Christ properly defined. And an even more critical issue is what will happen to the Sunday eucharistic assembly when "priestless parishes" become "priestless Sundays."

2. Implications for the Church Today

Some authors speak of the emergence of two different churches growing further and further apart. For example, Eugene Kennedy writes of two different cultures: a first culture of institutionality whose approach is literal and legal; and a second culture of the mystery of the people of God whose approach is metaphorical and sacramental.[2]

The recent Apostolic Exhortation on the Laity (*Christifideles Laici*) makes some telling points about the need for a complementarity of gifts within the *koinonia* of the Church. For example, para. #23 cautions against the indiscriminate use of the word "ministry" which could lead to a "clericalization" of the lay mission to the neglect of the "secular character" of lay faithful seeking to transform society. In times of necessity and expediency the lay faithful can be entrusted with "certain offices and roles that are connected with their pastoral ministry but do not require the character of orders." But such lay ministers are not to be considered pastors, a ministry which belongs to those in sacramental orders; rather their ministry is exercised in virtue of their baptism and specific lay vocation distinct from the sacred ministry.[3]

Yet in all candor this important principle spells little relief for the Church, given the declining number of priests worldwide. On the one hand, there exists the presumption of an almost unlimited reservoir of priests to continue "business as usual," although concessions are granted in exceptional circumstances. On the other hand, the local churches are pressed to rediscover a sense of a local community of faith calling forth new ministers as need arises. But what is the future of all this in view of the profound dislocation between the pastoral and sacramental ministry brought on by the priest crisis? Is the PLC a permanent situation or temporary and transitional to a further development? What is the future of lay ministry? What is the future of the ordained ministry? What is the future of the Eucharist as the center of Catholic Christian life?

Dean Hoge in his study, *The Future of Catholic Leadership*, presents eleven possible responses to the shortage of priests. He concludes that the most viable options are widening the eligibility criteria to include ordaining married men (option 6) and expanding the diaconate and lay ministries (option 11).[4] The former is currently not open for discussion; the latter has received some magisterial support from Rome in the recently promulgated *Directory for Sunday Celebrations in the Absence of a Priest* and will be under discussion by a commission to be appointed by the Holy Father. Will this option suffice to provide enough ecclesial ministers to serve the faith needs of the people of God in the future? And let us at the same time not forget to continue to recruit priestly vocations and to discern prayerfully the much-neglected and indispensable role of women in the Church.

3. The Tradition

The Church always has within it the resources to respond creatively to pastoral needs under the guidance of the Holy Spirit. Every diocese can recall its own early history of priests overseeing several faith communities as the Church expanded and grew. Every effort was made to provide Sunday Mass, for our tradition holds dear the primacy of the Sunday eucharistic assembly in Catholic life. On Sundays Catholic Christians assemble together to be formed into the people of God by word and sacrament. The Eucharist is indeed the sacrament of the unity of the Church, uniting the communicants of the local church with their bishop and through his communion with the bishop of Rome with the universal Church. Recent Roman documents testify to the centrality of the Eucharist in parish life, just short of articulating a right of the people to Sunday Mass.[5] The acute shortage of priests, however, is not going to make the Sunday eucharistic assembly a possibility for many Catholic Christians.

Fr. Gerard Broccolo has put forward his own challenging analysis of the crisis. There are four degrees of radical change. The first degree would be for bishops to ordain people to the priesthood who are not celibate or not male, who could thus preside at Eucharist and other sacramental celebrations. The second more radical degree of change would be for bishops to delegate others who hold public office, namely deacons, to preside at Eucharist. The third more radical degree would be for bishops to delegate those not in public office (laity) to preside at Eucharist. The most radical degree of change would be to do nothing at all. As a result, many local Christian communities would be without Sunday Eucharist as central to their life, or Christian communities would depute their own leadership, which is rampant congregationalism. This fourth degree represents the most radical departure from our 2000 years of a hierarchical tradition because it would "destroy Catholicism at its eucharistic core and spawn rampant congregationalism."[6]

4. Relationship to Other Developments

This past year I was fortunate to travel extensively: first to an ordination of two of our mission seminaries in Zaire, Africa in the summer of 1988; then a sabbatical from Seton Hall for the spring semester 1989 in order to observe the Church in the third world countries in South America and Asia. I witnessed the growing phenomenon of basic Christian communities: not just an outgrowth of liberation theology, but a core feature of the Church in most third world nations. In Zaire basic Christian communities meet weekly with their own cadre of lay ministries: leader, secretary, catechist, liturgist, and social concerns minister. A formation process prepares the lay ministers, and the parish priest carefully coordinates the groups who, as far as possible, meet under his presidency for Sunday Mass. In Chile there are basic Christian communities who meet on Sundays for Mass or a communion service. In Indonesia, where there is a natural societal breakdown into small groups, lay leaders or "pro-deacons" lead weekly communion services in 60% of the parishes. All this represents the response of third world countries to the scarcity of priests, which is to empower the laity and to provide Eucharist wherever possible. It is heartening to read that *Christifideles Laici* (#26) re-affirms the proposition of the synod fathers which suggests that in special circumstances parish structures are to be adapted and small Christian communities encouraged.

Thus the worldwide shortage of priests has necessitated the creation of new lay ministries and the formation of basic Christian communities (good news), but often with the attendant loss of a regular Sunday Eucharist (bad news).

5. Future Implications

Unless the number of ministerial priests increases dramatically, the usual manner of Sunday worship for many Catholic Christians will soon be conducted according to the norms of the *Directory for Sunday Celebrations in the Absence of a Priest*. The service consists of five components: introductory rites, liturgy of the word, thanksgiving, communion rites, and concluding rites. It is interesting to note that a recent survey taken by *U.S. Catholic* indicates a widespread dissatisfaction with this contingency solution.[7]

Attention will need to be given to the following issues:[8]

a. Difference between the Mass and the Sunday communion service

There are not the same thing! The *Directory* (#21) clearly states: "It is imperative that the faithful be taught to see the substitutional character of these celebrations, which should not be regarded as the optimal solution to new difficulties nor as a surrender to mere convenience." Already one hears such slips of the tongue as "priestless Masses," or "Sister's Mass," or "We like the way the lay people do Mass better." The unfortunate practice in many parishes of distributing holy communion from the tabernacle and not from the eucharistic elements consecrated on the altar has already set the stage for this misconception. Gabe Huck[9] and Robert Hovda[10] both suggest that to avoid confusion a far better solution would be to keep Sunday and to keep the assembly with the Liturgy of the Hours and the Lectionary readings, but to omit communion: the Eucharist should be missed.

b. Erosion of the ministerial priesthood

In many parts of the world there exists a whole new cadre of pastoral assistants who serve as leaders of local faith communities. They appear as "lay priests" because they exercise a number of priestly functions on the basis of wider delegation. They act as *de facto* leaders of communion services not always distinguishable by the simple laity from the full celebration of the Eucharist. This is related to the issue of role identity treated in response to the first question: coping with the shortage of priests by the creation of new ministries with the resulting role confusion of both.

c. Value of the word of God

The Second Vatican Council recognized the presence of Christ in the word. The exclusive use of communion services could imply that the presence of the Lord in his word has to be complemented by the sacrament in order to be sufficient. The resulting Sunday communion service is neither a celebration of the word, nor a eucharistic celebration, but a third entity in which even the sacrament is "fragmentalized." Moreover, Sunday communion services do not have a strong precedent in the tradition and seem to have first appeared in post-war East Germany when holy communion from the Sunday eucharistic assembly was brought to small groups of diaspora Christians.

d. Integral understanding of the Eucharist

The Eucharist is more than holy communion; it is the representation of the very mystery of Christ of which holy communion is an integral part. An exclusive use of communion services highlights the real (somatic) presence of Christ to the neglect of the commemorative actual presence of the work of redemption: the risen Christ offers himself through the hands of the ministerial priest in a ritual sacrifice in which all the faithful are invited to participate by their self-offering and commitment. The sacrament forms of the Lord's body and blood received at holy communion need to be seen as the fruit of the whole eucharistic action of memorial sacrifice.

6. Summary Reflections

To sum up, here are some reflections:

a. Dean Hoge contends that the "shortage of priests is an institutional problem, not a spiritual problem," which "can be solved through institutional measures."[11] This statement needs some nuancing and even correction. All too often we treat structural issues in the Church from an administrative standpoint, rather than with a spiritual vision. At the same time, a spiritual vision of the mystery of the Church and the future of ministry may call for institutional and administrative changes.

b. Is the PLC a permanent solution to the shortage of priests, or a temporary transition to a further unfolding of ministry in the Church whereby more of God's people will be called forth to ordained and non-ordained ministries? Could the good work of the PLC be living proof of the reservoir of talented men and women of faith who might eventually be called to sacramental orders in ways we do not yet clearly see? There is not a shortage of vocations in the

Church, only a shortage of vocations to the ministerial priesthood. Why is this so?

c. Preparation and catechesis of the people of God is necessary regarding their acceptance and expectations of the PLC. At the same time, lay people need to be challenged to further involve themselves in the mission of the Church both within the community of faith and in the world. This is not "volunteerism," but rather the activation of a mission inherent in the sacraments of Christian initiation.

d. Continued attention needs to be given to the special preparation and formation of the PLC, as the models clearly admit. There is some ambiguity about the place of the ordained deacon: sometimes he may serve as the PLC; at other times his is described as a "supportive pastoral role" assisting the PLC. Another issue is the role of lay people as PLCs, in addition to deacons and religious sisters already involved in this capacity. Hopefully places like the Greco Institute in Shreveport and the Institute for Pastoral Life will be able to attract future ecclesial ministers from the ranks of all the baptized, lay men and women alike. Further questions would then follow such as these: Full-time employment? Fair and equitable salary? How indigenous should the PLC be to the faith community served?

e. Whatever happens, collaborative ministry is the way of the future. Teamwork and consultation are going to be increasingly important. We do not need more fragmentation and alienation in the Church: any semblance of rivalry or competition between ministers ordained and non-ordained must be avoided. Ministry is about loving service, not power and control. All participate in the one priesthood of Jesus Christ, albeit in different ways. The distinctions that need to be made in terms of ministerial identity do not detract from the more basic commonality of "co-discipleship for the mission of the Church in the world."[12]

Notes

1. Dean Hoge, *The Future of Catholic Leadership: Responses to the Priest Shortage* (Kansas City: Sheed & Ward, 1987), pp. 105, 106.

2. Eugene Kennedy, *Tomorrow's Catholics, Yesterday's Church,* (New York: Harper & Row, 1988).

3. *Origins* (Feb. 9, 1989) vol. 18, no. 35, pp. 571, 572.

4. Dean Hoge, *The Future of Catholic Leadership,* pp. 207-216.

5. See canon 879 of the new *Code of Canon Law,* which begins a consideration of the Eucharist.

6. As cited in Dean Hoge, *The Future of Catholic Leadership,* pp. 212-215.

7. "Catholics won't settle for half a Mass." *U.S. Catholic* (June 1989), pp. 13-19. See also the survey conducted by the Bishops' Committee on the Liturgy reported in their *Newsletter* vol. xxiv (July-Aug., 1988) pp. 28-30.

8. See H.J. Graf, "Priestless Sunday Services with Communion and Resulting Problems. A Report on an Ongoing Controversy," *East Asian Pastoral Review* 18 (1981) pp. 175-189. Also William Marrevee, "'Priestless Masses'—At What Cost?", *Église et Théologie* 19 (1988), pp. 207-222.

9. Gabe Huck, "Priestless Sundays: Are We Looking or Leaping?" *Liturgy 80* (Oct. 1987), pp. 4,5.

10. Robert Hovda, "'Priestless Sundays' Reconsidered," *Worship* vol. 62, no. 2 (March 1988), pp. 154-159.

11. Dean Hoge, *The Future of Catholic Leadership,* p. xiii.

12. This felicitous phrase was coined by the four elected bishop delegates at the recent synod on the laity. See John L. May, Joseph L. Bernardin, *et al.,* "What We Have Heard, What We Will Say," *America,* 157 (Aug. 29- Sept. 5, 1987), p. 103.

Appendix C

Pastoral Extenders: Sociological Insights on the Pastoral Administrator's Role

Gary P. Burkart, Ph.D.

The church has always faced challenges in the execution of Christ's injunction to spread his message to all peoples. Every era has brought forth some problem in accomplishing the church's mission. Throughout the centuries of its existence, the church has had varying difficulties in providing adequately trained and prepared personnel to further its mission of preaching, teaching and ministering to the spiritual needs of its followers.

Within our own times, we witness a decline in ordained priests. While the number of Catholic parishioners and their parishes continues to increase, the number of priests and religious in the U.S. continues to decline. While these decline curves have moderated, projection of existing personnel twenty five years into the future leaves very little doubt that the church will not have enough ordained priests and religious to minister to people's religious needs. If the church's policies on celibate clergy and prohibition of women priests continue, then alternative methods of meeting pastoral needs must emerge or the church may witness a radical decline in its sacramental life. Some would argue that there is presently no shortage of vocations as numerous lay people are responding to these needs. The church is now in the middle of an evolutionary period in its history in which it struggles to give birth to alternate forms of ministry.

The emergence of the position of *pastoral administrator* in the American church has presented social scientists with a beautiful example of a social structure in evolution. The basic tools and concepts of the discipline are available to help make sense of and guide this process. One of the most fundamental conceptualizations used by social science is that of role. Role typically has had three meanings in social science: (a) role may be defined as the *structurally given demands* associated with a given social position, (b) likewise, role is seen as a person's *orientation or conception* of the part he or she enacts in the organization of group life, and finally, (c) role is defined as the *actions* of individual members as they participate in structured group life. Thus role is viewed as *role demands, role conception, and role performances*. (Cf Levinson in Coser and Rosenberg's *Sociological Theory*, 1964 for an elaboration upon the treatment of role found herein).

In highly institutionalized and routinized groups and organizations there may exist a high congruence between these three ways of defining a role. It is our contention that in a situation such as the American church faces today with the emerging shortage of ordained pastors for parishes (particularly in the rural and inner-city urban areas), these *three elements of a role may be highly incongruent*. We will now briefly explore each of these three in terms of our above argument.

Organizationally Given Role-Demands

Demands or expectations for our behavior, the role, are normally associated with a given position. In this case the role is the pastoral associate, pastoral administrator, the parish administrator, or the parish life coordinator. The fact that no consistent name exists attests that the church as an organization has yet to institutionalize an official position within its structure. It is a common assumption that the structural requirements for any social position are as a rule defined with a high degree of *explicitness, clarity and consensus*. In reality, we can find major differences and even contradictions in official norms from diocese to diocese, if they exist at all. Demands from an organization often lack unity and are multiple in nature.

Roles may have normative requirements that are more or less narrowly defined. Norms have an "ought" quality about them. They confer legitimacy and reward to certain behaviors and illegitimacy and punishment to others. When norms are not officially defined with specificity the organization is encouraging a great deal of individual personality variation in the performance of the role. However, in an evolutionary time such as we witness in today's church, such a relatively great input from personality need not be seen as necessarily a negative thing as it does encourage creativity and invention.

Individual's Orientations or Conceptions of the Role

A person's role definition may have varying degrees of fit with organizationally given role demands. In a time such as our own, we would expect some lack of fit between organizational expectations and personal orientations and conceptions of the role. A person's role conception is related to one's ideology of the organization of which one is a part, that is, a person's conception of its purposes, its modes of operation, and the prevailing forms of relationships. The function of a role conception is to offer an individual a definition and a rationale for one's position within the larger structure of the organization. Additionally, the individual's ideas about his/her occupational role are influenced by childhood experience, personality, formal and informal education. During this evolutionary period, the church must be prepared to have its parishioners, its hierarchy, and its pioneering *pastoral administrators* bring with them conceptualizations of this role that are influenced by these personal role definitions.

Role Behavior or Performance

Role performance refers to the more or less characteristic ways in which the individual *acts* as the occupant of a social position. A role is adequately performed when it follows accepted norms. A given role tells us individually how we are to *behave* with respect to interpersonal relations, authority figures, work and worship. Role performance, like any other form of human behavior, is the resultant of many forces. Some of these forces derive from the organization itself, such as the pressures of authority, informal group influences and sanctions. Others lie within the person, such as role conception and role experience.

Table 1

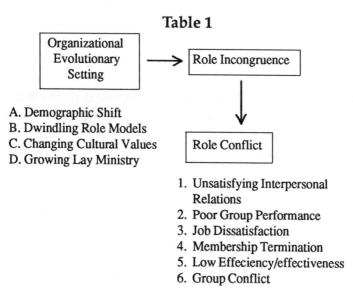

A. Demographic Shift
B. Dwindling Role Models
C. Changing Cultural Values
D. Growing Lay Ministry

1. Unsatisfying Interpersonal Relations
2. Poor Group Performance
3. Job Dissatisfaction
4. Membership Termination
5. Low Effeciency/effectiveness
6. Group Conflict

We posit that the church is experiencing a time in which a new position within its organizational apparatus appears to be evolving and that this position has yet to become institutionalized. Using role theory we would expect to find a lack of congruence between the three major facets of the role associated with this position. Organizational demands may not mesh well with the individual's conception of this new role, nor are the individual's role actions likely to be consistent with both the person's role conception and the bureaucratic role demands (Refer to Table 1). This is indeed a time in which both the corporate church and individual members of that body find themselves in a state of flux and ambiguity. This ambiguity may lead to anxiety, tension, burnout, and confusion for both the individuals and the church as a whole. Empirical studies have found role ambiguity and conflict in organizations to be associated with some or all of the following:

1. Unsatisfying interpersonal relations
2. Poor group performance
3. Job dissatisfaction
4. Membership termination
5. Low organizational efficiency and effectiveness, and
6. Group conflict (Refer to Table 2)

Table 2

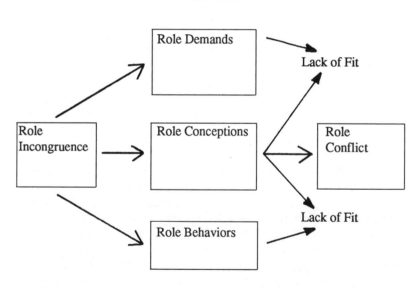

However, our era is replete with promise. Both the church and individuals can capitalize on this evolutionary process so that it leads to a greater congruence between the three elements of a role outlined above. In short, the official church needs to clarify its stance on *pastoral administrators* (when they are appropriate, for whom, etc.) so that it can be more explicit, clear, and consensual as to what the *pastoral administrator's* role is and what the role demands are that go with it. This may necessitate some clarification as to the roles in the larger structure of the church such as bishop, priest, pastor, parish and ordination. The individual persons who will serve as future *pastoral administrators* need to undergo formative experiences so that they will have conceptualizations of the *pastoral administrator's* role that offer definitions and rationales for this position that are reasonably consistent with the official church's role demands. Finally, these individuals need to evolve a way of doing pastoral administration that is consistent with their own role conceptions and the role demands of the church. One aspect of pastoral planning at all levels is to work toward a smoother coordination of the three aspects of the *pastoral administrator's* role as introduced here. Only when the non-local levels of the Church present a clearer vision of what it is to be a bishop, a priest, or a pastor in today's parishes and promulgate a more focused statement of ministry and ministers can we expect the role of *pastoral administrator* to become more consensual, explicit, and clear. However, if we see the growth of new ministries in pastoral work in the parish as a revitalization movement, then the local church has a role to play in calling the non-local church to define what these new ministries are adn what ministers are needed to execute them.

In preparation for the 1989 symposium on Parish leadership, I studied five cases of parishes led by *pastoral administrators* (referred to in the symposium as parish life coordinators). Each case exemplified a variation on the role. Systematic analysis reveals that practices common to all five models lead to a great deal of unnecessary role incongruence and conflict. We would like to present some of these practices or weaknesses. It seems clear that not all dioceses have faced the challenge that the decline in ordained priests is presenting to them. In several of the case studies it is not clear to the *pastoral administrators* out of which diocesan ministries *pastoral administration* came. Dioceses must not only have *pastoral administration* policies to bring about a minimum of consistency between parishes, but *pastoral adminstration* plans that tell all in the diocese what the diocesan attitudes are about pastoral administration, what the human resource needs for pastoring are and will be in the future, and some plans around which parishes may prepare for *administration* in their future. Many models fail to adequately prepare the parish, the people, the clergy and all involved. This probably results from a lack of a well-thought out diocesan plan to meet pastoral needs. Lack of parish/diocesan planning may likewise mean that last minute plans are sprung on unsuspecting parishioners.

A well-developed policy stating qualifications for hiring, screening processes, salary, benefits, termination agreements and the like is missing in some of the cases. A parish policy coordinated with a diocesan policy would seem to be essential to a smooth operating program within any diocese. Such a plan must state the parish's expectations for the *pastoral administrator* and leave little doubt on the part of either the parishioners or the *administrator* as to what is expected.

Across models, one final problem area lies in the integration of the *pastoral administrator* into the *pastoral administration* of the diocese. The *PA* should find support, guidance and encouragement at all levels of operations within the diocese. Support groups and human relations sensitivity are needed to adequately integrate *PA's* into existing pastoral groups in the diocese.

Elements Needed in any Parish Situation

I presented a model for parish transition at an IPL Symposium in the Fall of 1987, (Cf. *Continuing the Journey: Parishes in Transition*, Leader's Manual, 1987). With a few modifications this model can serve dioceses in need of Parish Life Coordinator plans. The model proposed four stages: (1) Stage I—Diagnosing the Problem; (2) Stage II—Assessing Parish Motivations and Capacity to Change; (3) Stage III—Implementing the Change Processes, and (4) Stage IV—Institutionalizing Change. This model if applied would reduce or eliminate most of the role incongruence or conflict presently existing in many parishes. These steps would make *role demands* more consensual, explicit, and clear. *Pastoral administrators* would have *role conceptions* consistent with role demands. Finally, various *pastoral administrators'* actual *role behaviors* would be more isomorphic to both role demands and role conceptions. The following are elaborations on how each stage of such a plan might do these things.

Stage I—*Diagnosing the Problem*

At this stage every diocese needs to do basic research and planning with its parishes in terms of human and financial planning. The diocese should project personnel over a 20 year period into the future. Likewise, the diocese needs to take a 20 year view of its financial resources. A second kind of diocesan planning would involve ascertaining individual parish and diocesan-wide pastoral needs. For example, the Diocese of Rochester has found out that the number of pastors to parishes will be .5 in another ten years. Such dioceses must plan now as to which of the parishes are in need of pastoral extenders and what types of solutions are possible by what period in the future. Each parish should have some planning process similar to that of the diocese so that it can begin to come to grips with its present and future pastoral needs. Parishioners, parishes, priests and diocesan functionaries would all then have a good view of their needs through time. Using creative problem structuring, future scenarios and goal setting, parishes should not be getting surprise phone calls telling them that they will have no pastor for the next year.

Stage II—*Assessing Parish for Change*

Parishes that may need pastoral extenders in terms of the above plans should be encouraged to explore their attitudes toward such a development. What kind of change is the parish willing to accept now? What kinds of changes may need to be encouraged for the future?

Stage III—*Implementing the Change Process*

Parishes in tune with their diocesan pastoral needs plan for the future may realize that they must prepare for some sort of pastoral extender role. Using a diocesan *pastoral administration* plan and their own assessment of their capacity for change, the parish should undergo a process of role clarification long before the resident pastor leaves. The ideal would be for a year or more of internship by a person who will take over coordination of the parish at some point in the future.

The diocese should sponsor or make available training programs that would turn out adequately prepared *pastoral administrators*. Carefully spelled out *pastoral administration* policies modelled on that of the diocese, but taking into account local needs, should be present to guide the selection of a person for the *PA* internship. This would be followed by an official appointment and installation. Provisions for termination and reappointment in another parish would be included in such a policy.

Stage IV—*Institutionalizing Change*

Diocesan and parish plans and policies for *pastoral administration* must provide a mechanism to periodically evaluate the degree to which they are meeting the needs of both the parish and the diocese. Processes to change such plans and policies must be provided to accommodate the learning that takes place as this new role becomes more institutionalized. Finally, the parish through its council and the diocese through its pastoral groups and councils must find ways to offer support to pastoral extenders by integrating them fully with whatever groups and functions exist relevant to pastoring. If such support groups do not exist, the diocese should be instrumental in their creation of the creation of other support mechanisms.

It is believed that models incorporating the above-mentioned four steps will do much to eliminate the role conflict we see inherent in the newly-emerging role of *pastoral administrator*. These policies and plans at both diocesan and parish levels will make clear the role demands for such a job. Likewise role conceptions of various *pastoral administrators* would begin to become congruous through adequate formation program and the actual role performances of *pastoral administrators* would become more consistent between individuals occupying this position.

Institutionalization of the role of *pastoral administrator* (or some role yet to be evolved) should reduce or eliminate most of the inefficiences found in contemporary models of *parish administration*. With such inefficiences removed, the church will be better equipped to evaluate existing models and to suggest needed models. Questions about the effectiveness and efficiency of any one of these models can be assessed by empirical study. Furthermore, each model can be examined for its ecclesiological and pastoral implications. Whether one wants to evaluate models such as those delineated in The National Pastoral Life Center's paper entitled *Alternate Staffing of Parishes*, 1987, the reduction of role ambiguity presently found in parts of the church will make such a task much easier. Factors such as locale, local culture, readiness of the parish as well as ecclesiological considerations could then be applied in making decisions as to which model should be used.

In the final analysis, the church will more than likely have to call upon many models, having worked out of them some of the inefficiencies noted in this work. It is likely that we will come to admit the wisdom of a pluralism of pastoral method in our endeavor to bring Christ to the world.

Selected Bibliography

Congregation for Divine Worship, *Directory for Sunday Celebrations in the Absence of a Priest*. Vatican City, June 2, 1988.

Gallagher, Maureen, *Parishes in Transition*. Kansas City: Sheed and Ward, 1986.

Graf, H.J., "Priestless Sunday Services with Communion and Resulting Problems: A Report on an Ongoing Controversy." *East Asian Pastoral Review* 18 (1981) pp. 175-189.

Hoge, Dean, *Future of Catholic Leadership: Responses to the Priest Shortage*. Kansas City: Sheed and Ward, 1987.

Huck, Gabe, "Priestless Sundays: Are We Looking or Leaping?," *Liturgy 80* (Oct. 1987), pp. 4-5.

John Paul II, *Christifideles Laici*. In *Origins* (Feb. 9, 1989), vol. 18, no. 35.

Marrevee, William, "'Priestless Masses'—At What Cost," *Église et Théologie 19* (1988) pp. 207-222.

Monette, Maurice L., *Partners in Ministry: Priests in Collaboration with Parish Life Coordinators*. Kansas City: Sheed and Ward, 1988.

National Pastoral Life Center, "Alternate Staffing of Parishes," in *Center Papers: A Resource for Diocesan Leadership*, New York, N.Y.: National Pastoral Life Center, 1987.

Osborne, Kenan, *Priesthood: A History of the Ordained Ministry in the Roman Catholic Church*. New York/Mahwah: Paulist Press, 1989.

Other Titles from IPL:

Books

PARTNERS IN MINISTRY
Priests in Collaboration with Parish Life Coordinators
Maurice L. Monette, editor $4.95
CONTINUING THE JOURNEY
Parishes in Transition, Maureen Gallagher, editor
Participant's Book $5.95
Leader's Manual $4.95

Videos

STEWARDSHIP OF TREASURES
A Response to the Financial Challenges of Today's Parish
featuring Msgr. Joseph Champlin $39.95
THE RURAL PARISH
Its Unique Qualities
featuring Br. David Andrews, Dr. Patricia O'Connell Killen,
and Fr. David O'Connor $39.95
PRIESTS IN COLLABORATION
WITH PARISH LIFE COORDINATORS
featuring Bishop John McRaith and Msgr. Andrew Cusack . . . $39.95
LAY PRESIDERS IN LITURGY
The Experience and the Questions $39.95
CANON LAW AND THE PARISH
featuring Rev. Edward G. Pfnausch, JCL
Tape I:
General Introduction and Foundations for Church Law $49.95
Tape II:
Law and Theology and Interpretation of Canon Law $49.95
Tape III:
Fundamental Rights and the Sanctity Mission $49.95
PARISHES IN TRANSITION
Preparing for New Forms of Pastoral Leadership
featuring Maureen Gallagher $39.95
CANON LAW AND PARISH MINISTRY:
The Shape and Mission of the Parish as a Ministering Community
featuring Rev. Edward G. Pfnausch $39.95

Available from: Sheed & Ward
                 115 E. Armour Blvd.
                 P.O. Box 419492
                 Kansas City, MO 64141

To order, call: 1-800-33-7373